Classic
CHICKEN DISHES

Sue Ashworth • Jennie Berresford • Judy Bowen • Judy Bugg
Carole Handslip • Jane Hartshorn • Kathryn Hawkins
Cara Hobday • Deh-ta Hsiung • Louise Steele
Rosemary Wadey • Pamela Westland

SMITHMARK

This edition published in the USA in 1997 by SMITHMARK Publishers,
a division of U.S. Media Holdings Inc.,
16 East 32nd Street, New York, NY 10016

SMITHMARK books are available for bulk purchase for sales promotion and premium
use. For details write or call the manager of special sales, SMITHMARK Publishers,
16 East 32nd Street, New York, NY 10016; (212) 532–6800.

ISBN: 0-7651-9481-3

Edited, designed and produced by Haldane Mason, London

Acknowledgements
Editor: Christine McFadden
Design: Digital Artworks Partnership Ltd
Photography: Karl Adamson, Sue Atkinson, Iain Bagwell, Martin Brigdale,
Amanda Heywood, Joff Lee, Patrick McLeavey and Clive Streeter
Home Economists: Sue Ashworth, Jennie Berresford, Joanna Craig, Jill Eggleton,
Nicola Fowler, Carole Handslip, Jane Hartshorn, Kathryn Hawkins, Cara Hobday,
Deh-ta Hsiung, Wendy Lee, Louise Steele, Rosemary Wadey, Pamela Westland
Additional Recipes: Cara Hobday
Additional Photography: Iain Bagwell

Printed in Italy

Material in this book has previously appeared in *Balti Cooking, Barbecues,
Cajun & Creole Cooking, Caribbean Cooking, Chinese Cantonese Cooking,
Chinese Szechuan Cooking, Classic Home Cooking, Classic Indian Cooking,
The Complete Book of Italian Cooking, Cooking For One & Two,
Cooking On A Budget, Hot & Cold Sandwiches, Italian Regional Cooking,
Low-Fat Cooking, Mexican Cooking, Pasta Dishes, Picnics,
Quick & Easy Indian Cooking, Quick & Easy Meals,
Recipes with Yogurt, Sensational Salads, Soups & Broths, Thai Cooking,
Thai Side Dishes* and *Wok Cooking.*

Note
Cup measurements in this book are for American cups.
Tablespoons are assumed to be 15 ml. Unless otherwise stated, milk is assumed to be
full-fat, eggs are AA extra large and pepper is freshly ground black pepper.

CONTENTS

INTRODUCTION 6

APPETIZERS & SNACKS 11

Oriental Chicken Salad 12 • Chicken, Papaya & Avocado Salad 13 • Veronica Salad 14
Chicken Pasta Provençale 15 • Chicken Liver & Watercress Pâté 16 • Potted Chicken 17 • Chicken in Pita Bread 18
Super Club Sandwich 19 • Spiced Chicken Koftas 20 • Thai Chicken Egg Rolls 21 • Chicken "Scallops" 22

SOUPS 23

Chicken & Corn Soup 24 • Chicken Soup with Almonds 25
Chicken & Garbanzo Bean Soup 26 • Cock-a-Leekie Soup 27 • Chicken & Chestnut Soup 28
Chicken & Corn Chowder 29 • Noodles in Soup 30 • Hot & Sour Soup 31 • Chicken & Noodle One-Pot 32

LIGHT MEALS 33

Spiced Chicken & Grape Salad 34 • Chicken with Lemon & Tarragon 35 • Bang-Bang Chicken 36
Thai-Style Chicken-Fried Rice 37 • Crunchy-Topped Chicken/Spiced Chicken Salad 38 • Chicken & Ham Pie 39
Raised Chicken Pie 40 • Three Meat Package 41 • Chicken & Corn Puff 42
Tagliatelle with Chicken & Almonds 43 • Chicken-Filled Tortellini 44 • Pasta Medley 45 • Chicken Fajitas 46
Enchilada Layers 47 • Chicken Burritos 48

SAUTÉS & STIR-FRIES 49

Chicken Kiev 50 • Skillet-Cooked Chicken & Artichokes 51 • Chicken Paprika 52
Chicken & Almond Rissoles with Stir-Fried Vegetables 53 • Chicken, Cilantro, Ginger & Lemon Stir-Fry 54
Chicken with Peanut Sauce 55 • Chicken with Mushrooms 56 • Chicken with Bell Pepper 57
Chicken with Celery & Cashew Nuts 58 • Quick Chinese Chicken with Noodles 59
Lime & Cilantro Chicken-Fried Rice 60

BROILS, GRILLS & ROASTS 61

Sticky Chicken Wings 62 • Lemon & Mint Chicken Burgers 63 • Barbecued Chicken 64
Chicken in Spicy Yogurt 65 • Chargrilled Chicken Salad 66 • Mediterranean Grilled Chicken 67 • Spicy Chicken Tikka 68
Chicken Tikka & Mango Kabobs 69 • Tandoori Chicken 70 • Sesame Skewered Chicken with Ginger Baste 71
Crispy Chicken Drumsticks 72 • Chicken Satay Kabobs 73 • Blackened Chicken with Guacamole 74
Jerk Chicken 75 • Filipino Chicken 76 • Thai Chicken with Peanut Sauce 77 • Crispy-Coated Squab Chickens 78
Squab Chickens with Green Peppercorns 79 • Traditional Roast Chicken 80

CASSEROLES 81

Chicken Cacciatora 82 • Chicken with 40 Garlic Cloves 83 • Chicken & Black-Eyed Peas 84
Chicken & Chili Bean Pot 85 • Chicken with Green Olives 86 • Roman Chicken 87 • Coq au Vin Blanc 88
Country Chicken Casserole 89 • Chicken with Rice & Peas 90 • Chicken & Vegetable Rice 91 • Jambalaya 92
Baton Rouge Chicken Gumbo 93 • Chicken Etouffé 94 • Grillades with Grits 95

INDEX 96

INTRODUCTION

The 19th-century French gastronome Brillat-Savarin was right when he wrote "Poultry is for the cook what canvas is to the painter." When it comes to cooking chicken, the options are endless. Depending on the size of the bird and the cut, chicken can be stir-fried, sautéd, grilled, broiled, baked, roasted, or casseroled. However you choose to cook it, there's no doubt that chicken gets top marks for versatility.

It's hardly surprising, therefore, chicken has an established presence in every national cuisine. Descended from a Malaysian jungle fowl known as a mound bird, chickens were first domesticated in the Indus valley as long ago as 2500 B.C., although they did not find their way to the Western world until much later. The Romans are said to have incubated huge quantities of eggs kept warm with the steam from hot underground springs—their knowledge of central heating must certainly have helped with this. We have the Romans to thank for the invention of the capon—a large male bird with succulent, tasty flesh. They circumvented a law forbidding the consumption of fattened chickens, which were a much-loved delicacy, by castrating cockerels. These emasculated birds grew to twice their normal size but without any loss of flavor.

Ease of rearing and the eggs produced must have contributed to the chicken's universal popularity, but there's little doubt that its value lay in the amazing variety of dishes to which it was suited. The French *poule au pot* is a homely chicken and vegetable casserole, fragrant with herbs and wine. Tandoori chicken, an Indian specialty, is made with skinless, jointed chicken marinated in yogurt and spices before roasting in the fierce heat of the tandoor oven. The Italians like to sauté chicken joints with tomatoes and garlic, or grill whole baby chickens spatchcock-style over a rosemary-scented wood fire. In the Middle East, a whole chicken is slowly simmered with nuts or dried fruit. In Southeast Asia small boneless chunks of chicken are stir-fried with fragrant aromatics such as ginger, chilies, lemongrass, and garlic.

Tasty, nutritious, and easy on the pocket and waistline, chicken is the perfect choice for family meals, special occasion dinners, parties, barbecues, and picnics. It's packed with protein and B vitamins, and, if you trim off the skin, it contains very little fat—three ounces of lean flesh contains only 147 calories.

On the following pages you'll discover for yourself a marvelous selection of classic chicken dishes to add to your repertoire. The recipes include old favorites, such as Traditional Roast Chicken, Coq au Vin, and Chicken Kiev, as well as less familiar but nevertheless classic creations from around the world. Try Baton Rouge Chicken Gumbo from the Deep South, or Bang-Bang Chicken from China, or Chicken with 40 Garlic Cloves from France. Whatever your level of skill, the easy-to-follow, step-by-step directions will guarantee you success every time.

BUYING GUIDE

*When buying fresh chicken, check that it is chilled
and any packaging is not torn or broken. Make sure frozen chicken is
still frozen solid. Look for the United States Department of Agriculture (USDA)
quality inspection stamp. The highest grade, U.S. Grade A, covers most of the whole
birds and pieces sold in supermarkets. Chickens with this grade on the label have
a good shape and appearance, are full-fleshed, and free from defects. Some individual
states have an additional inspection mark.*

All-natural chicken This is a USDA-approved term that requires any injections the bird receives to be 100 percent natural, such as salt and water, but not sodium phosphate. The term does not put any restrictions on the bird's diet or living conditions.

Bresse chicken Reared in Bresse, in the Burgundy region of France, these birds are rated as having the most superior flavor by countless chefs all over the world. They are reared in free-range conditions on high-quality natural feed. They are expensive and available only from gourmet food stores and delicatessens.

Broiler-fryers These birds are reared to produce tender flesh, and usually weigh about 3½ pounds, although you will find some weighing up to 5 pounds. They are best jointed and broiled or fried, but whole birds can also be roasted, steamed, or casseroled.

Capon These are large, castrated roosters that can weigh as much as 10 pounds. They have a large proportion of white meat and the flesh is delicately marbled with fat which gives it an excellent flavor, especially when roasted. A capon makes a good alternative to turkey for a special occasion.

Cornish game hen Also known as rock Cornish hens, these are small chickens that weigh about 1½ pounds, with tender flesh. Each bird will serve two persons.

Free-range chicken USDA regulations specify that a "free-range" bird must have access to the outdoors. The labeling doesn't specify what the bird is fed.

Fresh chicken Birds labeled as "fresh" at the supermarket will not have been frozen, but they may contain ice crystals. This is because they can be transported and stored at temperatures from 36° to 0°F. USDA regulations only consider poultry frozen when the temperature falls below zero.

Stewing chickens These are mature female birds that generally weigh up to 5 pounds. They have a good flavor, and are ideal for the casserole or for making stock. The flesh is too tough for roasting or broiling.

Squab chicken Known as *poussin* in French, these are 4- to 6-week-old chickens weighing no more than 1½ pounds. They are best broiled, grilled or roasted.

Roasting chicken These weigh about 5 pounds. They are best roasted whole, but if they are not too large, they can be jointed and used for frying or broiling.

FOOD SAFETY

Chicken is very prone to contamination by salmonella bacteria, which can cause serious food poisoning.

- After buying, take your chicken home quickly, preferably in a freezer bag or cool box.

- Return frozen birds immediately to the freezer.

- Cover loosely with foil and store on the bottom shelf of the refrigerator for no more than one or two days, depending on the sell-by date.

- Frozen birds should be thoroughly thawed before using. Do not thaw at room temperature. If time permits, allow 5 hours per pound to thaw a whole bird in the refrigerator. Alternatively, thaw the bird, in its wrappings, in a sink of cold water. Allow 30 minutes per pound and change the water frequently.

- Always wash any equipment, your hands, and the work surface with soapy water after you have handled raw chicken.

Chicken must always be cooked all the way through. You should never partially cook chicken with the idea of completing cooking later on. This is because bacteria can multiply at an alarming rate in a very short period of time. To test for doneness, insert a skewer into the thickest part of the thigh—the juices should run clear without the slightest hint of pink. If they are not clear, return the bird to the oven and test again after 5 minutes.

COOKING CHICKEN

Chicken is one of the most versatile foods and it can be cooked in a variety of ways.

Sautéing and pan-frying
Small thighs and joints can be fried in about 1½ inches of peanut oil in a large skillet. Heat the oil to 350°F, or test by putting a cube of bread into the hot oil: If it browns in 1 minute, the oil is hot enough. Fry the chicken pieces on all sides, with or without a coating of seasoned flour, until they are an even golden brown. Then reduce the heat and fry for 20 to 30 minutes longer until the juices run clear when the chicken is pierced with the tip of a knife. The exact cooking time depends on size and thickness. Drain well on crumpled paper towels before serving.

Stir-frying
The key to successful stir-frying is to cut boneless meat into similar-sized strips, small cubes or thin slices. This guarantees the meat will cook evenly and remain juicy. Heat the wok or a skillet before adding a small amount of peanut oil. When the oil starts to smoke, add the chicken pieces and stir-fry with your chosen flavorings for 3 to 4 minutes until cooked through. Other ingredients can be stir-fried at the same time. Or, the chicken can be stir-fried by itself, then removed from the wok while you stir-fry the remaining ingredients. Return the chicken to the pan briefly when the other ingredients are cooked.

Broiling
Broiling is a sure-fire method of bringing out the best in chicken. The intense heat of the broiler quickly seals the juicy, succulent flesh beneath a golden, crispy exterior. Although the technique appears simple, success depends on speed, timing, correct distance from the heat source, and good-quality ingredients. If you broil at too high a temperature and too close to the heat source, for example, the outside of the chicken will be burned before the inside is cooked. Too little heat for too long will dry the flesh out. The chicken should be placed 4 to 6 inches away from a medium heat. Young birds, such as Cornish game hens or small roasters, are the most suitable candidates for broiling as these are least likely to dry out and become too tough.

To brown the skin evenly, the meat should be reasonably flat and compact. Even a small whole chicken needs to be cut into joints, or split down the backbone and flattened, a technique known as spatchcocking. The heat then penetrates the flesh evenly. Chicken quarters are best cut into smaller pieces for broiling. Divide leg portions into thighs and drumsticks. Breast meat, which can be slightly dry and dense, is best divided into bite-sized chunks for kabobs, or sliced and pounded flat. Wings are perfect for speedy broiling as the bones disperse the heat and the skin traps moisture, making a very succulent dish.

Roasting

With crisp, golden-brown skin and moist succulent meat, a perfectly roasted chicken is an all-time delight. The best chickens for roasting usually weigh about 5 pounds. When you're ready to cook the chicken, remove any lumps of fat from the opening to the body cavity. Rinse the bird inside and out under cold running water, then pat it dry with paper towels. Season the cavity generously with salt and freshly ground black pepper. Insert any stuffing you may be using into the neck cavity just before putting the bird in the oven. Extra stuffing can be cooked in a lightly greased baking dish covered in foil. Place the bird on a rack in a roasting pan, then brush the skin all over with oil or melted butter, or rub with softened butter. Baste the bird two or three times with the pan juices during roasting. Alternatively, if you cover the chicken with a piece of cheesecloth dipped in melted butter, you won't need to baste at all. Check the chicken is thoroughly cooked by inserting a skewer into the thickest part of the leg. The juices should run clear without a trace of pink.

Casseroling

Casseroling, otherwise known as braising, is an easy-to-learn culinary technique in which the meat, vegetables, seasonings, and cooking liquid are gently simmered in the oven or over the lowest possible heat in a deep pan or a casserole with a tight-fitting lid. The technique is particularly delectable with chicken and is a good method for cooking larger, mature birds as it tenderizes the meat and the cooking juices can be reduced to make a wonderful sauce. The chicken is usually jointed, although small birds can be cooked whole if you have a deep enough pot. Season the chicken and brown it all over in butter or hot oil, or a mixture of both. Pour in a liquid, such as stock, wine, or water, or a mixture, together with any other ingredients. Cover and simmer gently on the stovetop or in the oven for about 1 hour until the chicken is meltingly tender and cooked through.

APPETIZERS & SNACKS

Infinitely versatile, cold chicken is the ideal standby for delicious and imaginative appetizers. Brought to life with Oriental dressings or tropical fruits, chicken salad makes the perfect light lunch for the calorie-conscious, or an appetizing first course. Chicken livers and dark leg meat can be turned into richly flavored pâtés and potted meats to start a meal or to serve on a picnic. When it comes to sandwiches, it's hard to beat a triple-decker chicken club sandwich, although Middle Eastern pita bread stuffed with spicy chicken and a salad also hits the spot. Tender and moist, cooked chicken is a universal ingredient in countless snacks from all over the world.

CHICKEN IN PITA BREAD (PAGE 18)

ORIENTAL CHICKEN SALAD

Mirin, soy sauce, and sesame oil give an Oriental flavor to this delicious salad.

SERVES 4

INGREDIENTS:
*4 skinless, boneless chicken breast
    halves
1/3 cup mirin or sweet sherry
1/3 cup light soy sauce
1 tbsp sesame oil
3 tbsp olive oil
1 tbsp red-wine vinegar
1 tbsp Dijon mustard
8 ounces egg noodles
8 ounces bean sprouts
3 1/2 cups shredded Chinese leaves
2 scallions, sliced
3 1/2 cups sliced mushrooms*

1 Pound the chicken breast halves out to an even thickness between two sheets of plastic wrap with a rolling pin or cleaver.

2 ▲ Put the chicken in a roasting pan. Combine the mirin and soy sauce and brush the mixture over the chicken. Roast in a preheated oven, 400°F, 20 to 30 minutes, basting often. Remove from the oven and let cool slightly.

3 ▼ Meanwhile, combine the oils and vinegar with the mustard.

4 ▼ Cook the noodles. Rinse under cold running water, then drain and immediately toss in the dressing.

5 ▼ Toss the bean sprouts, Chinese leaves, scallions, and mushrooms with the noodles.

6 Slice the cooked chicken very thinly and stir into the noodles. Serve the salad immediately.

CHICKEN, PAPAYA & AVOCADO SALAD

Try this recipe with peaches or nectarines instead of papaya.

SERVES 4

INGREDIENTS:
4 skinless, boneless chicken breast halves
1 red chili, seeded and chopped
$1^2/_3$ tbsp red-wine vinegar
$^1/_3$ cup olive oil
1 papaya, peeled
1 avocado, peeled
4 ounces alfalfa sprouts
4 ounces bean sprouts
salt and pepper

4 ▼ Slice the papaya and avocado to the same thickness as the chicken. Arrange on four plates with the chicken, alfalfa sprouts, and bean sprouts. Serve with the dressing.

3 ▲ Place the chicken breast halves on a chopping board. Using a very sharp knife, cut each one across the grain into thin diagonal slices; set aside.

1 ▼ Poach the chicken in boiling water 15 minutes, or until cooked through. Remove with a slotted spoon, set aside to cool.

2 ▼ Combine the chili, vinegar, and oil, and season well; set aside.

VERONICA SALAD

A delicious salad consisting of strips of cooked chicken with grapes, celery, and hard-cooked eggs in a lightly curried, mint dressing garnished with Belgian endive.

SERVES 6

INGREDIENTS:
*4 skinless, boneless chicken breast
    halves
2 tbsp olive oil
1 tbsp sunflower oil
1 to 2 garlic cloves, crushed
1 onion, finely chopped
2 tbsp chopped fresh mint
4 green celery stalks
1½ cups black grapes, preferably
    seedless
1 cup large green seedless grapes
2 tbsp butter or margarine
1 tbsp all-purpose flour
½ tsp curry powder
3 tbsp white wine or stock
5 tbsp milk
2 tbsp plain yogurt
2 tbsp mayonnaise
1 head Belgian endive
2 hard-cooked eggs
salt and pepper*

1 ▼ Cut the chicken into thin strips. Heat the oils in a skillet. Add the garlic and chicken, and fry gently until well sealed. Add the onion and fry until the chicken and onion are tender. Stir in the mint and add salt and pepper. Drain off the oil and juices. Put the chicken mixture into a bowl and leave until cold.

2 ▲ Cut the celery into thin diagonal slices. Reserve a few whole black grapes for garnish. If they are large or contain seeds, cut the remainder in half and remove any seeds. Add to the salad with the celery and the green grapes.

3 Melt the butter or margarine in a pan. Stir in the flour and curry powder and cook 1 to 2 minutes. Add the wine or stock and the milk and bring to a boil. Simmer until thick. Remove the pan from the heat. Season and stir in the yogurt. Cover with plastic wrap and leave until cool.

4 ▼ Stir the mayonnaise into the cool sauce. Add to the chicken mixture, tossing to coat. Spoon into a serving dish. Cut the Belgian endive leaves into 2-inch pieces and arrange around the edge of the salad with the reserved grapes and hard-cooked egg quarters. Cover and chill until ready to serve.

CHICKEN PASTA PROVENCALE

Use any pasta shape for this salad, but drain it thoroughly so the cooking water does not dilute the dressing.

SERVES 4

INGREDIENTS:
6 ounces dried pasta shapes
2 tbsp olive oil
12 ounces skinless, boneless chicken
  breast, cut into strips
2 zucchini, sliced
1 red bell pepper, seeded and cut into
  chunks
2 garlic cloves, sliced
4 tomatoes, cut into wedges
1 can (2-ounce) anchovies, drained and
  chopped
$1/4$ cup ripe olives, stoned and
  halved
sprig of fresh parsley, to garnish

FRENCH DRESSING:
3 tbsp olive oil
1 tbsp wine vinegar
1 garlic clove, crushed
$1/2$ tsp Dijon or Meaux mustard
1 tsp clear honey
salt and pepper

1 Cook the pasta in boiling salted water 10 to 12 minutes until "al dente". Drain thoroughly.

2 Whisk all the dressing ingredients together until thoroughly blended.

3 ▲ Put the pasta into a large bowl. Add 4 tablespoons of the French dressing and stir together.

4 Heat the oil in a skillet. Add the chicken and stir-fry 4 to 5 minutes, stirring occasionally, until cooked. Remove the chicken from the pan.

5 ▼ Add the zucchini, bell pepper, and garlic to the pan. Fry 12 to 15 minutes, stirring, until softened.

6 ▲ Add the chicken, fried vegetables, tomatoes, anchovies, and olives to the pasta. Mix together so all the ingredients are blended.

7 Transfer to a serving dish and garnish with parsley. Serve immediately while warm.

CHICKEN LIVER & WATERCRESS PATE

The peppery flavors of the watercress really come through in this soft pâté— serve it on hot melba toast as a delicious snack, or for a first course.

SERVES 4 TO 6

INGREDIENTS:
4 tbsp butter
1 onion, chopped
8 ounces chicken livers, chopped
1 garlic clove, chopped
4 ounces watercress, trimmed and chopped
1 tbsp chopped fresh thyme
1 tbsp chopped fresh parsley
1 tbsp dry sherry
salt and pepper
sprig of watercress, to garnish

1 ▼ Melt the butter in a skillet. Add the onion and fry gently about 5 minutes until soft.

2 ▼ Add the chicken livers and garlic and fry gently 3 to 4 minutes until the livers are cooked through.

3 ▲ Remove the pan from the heat; set aside to cool slightly. Stir in the watercress, fresh herbs, sherry, salt, and pepper.

4 ▼ Transfer the mixture to a food processor and process until the chicken livers are finely chopped, but still have some texture—alternatively, put the mixture through a food mill.

5 Transfer the mixture to a serving dish. Cover and refrigerate until chilled. Serve with hot melba toast.

POTTED CHICKEN

Cooked poultry, meat, and game can all be prepared in this traditional way—finely ground and cooked with onions, spices, and sherry or port wine. Serve as a first course or a sandwich filling.

SERVES 4 TO 6

INGREDIENTS:

8 ounces boneless cooked chicken leg meat (or any boneless game, beef, or lamb)
½ cup butter
1 onion, chopped very finely
1 to 2 garlic cloves, crushed
2 tbsp sherry or port wine
about 4 tbsp stock
good pinch of ground mace, nutmeg, or allspice
pinch of Italian seasoning
salt and pepper
sprigs of fresh thyme, to garnish

TO SERVE:

sprigs of watercress
cherry tomatoes or tomato wedges
crusty bread or toast

1 ▼ Remove any skin or gristle from the poultry, game, or meat. Finely grind twice through a meat grinder, or finely chop in a food processor.

2 Melt half the butter in a saucepan. Add the onion and garlic and fry gently until soft but only lightly colored.

3 Stir the chicken into the pan, followed by the sherry or port wine and just enough of the stock to moisten the mixture. Season to taste with salt, pepper, mace, and herbs.

4 ▲ Press the mixture into a lightly greased serving dish or several individual dishes and level the top. Cover and chill until firm.

5 ▲ Melt the remaining butter and pour a thin layer over the potted chicken. Add a few sprigs of thyme and chill thoroughly so the herbs set in the butter.

6 Serve spooned onto plates, or in individual pots on plates, garnished with watercress, tomatoes, and crusty bread or toast.

CHICKEN IN PITA BREAD

Pita bread makes a great container for fast and flavorsome meals—either on the move or for a weekend lunch.

SERVES 4

INGREDIENTS:
1 tbsp cumin seed, crushed
1 tbsp coriander seed, crushed
1 tbsp ground turmeric
1 tbsp black mustard seed
2 tsp chili flakes
1/4 cup olive oil
1 1/2 pounds skinless, boneless chicken
1 1/4 cups plain yogurt
3 ounces fresh cilantro
3 ounces fresh mint
juice of 1 lime
sprig of flat-leafed parsley
salt and pepper

TO SERVE:
4 pita breads
salad greens
cucumber slices
cherry tomatoes

1 ▼ Combine the cumin, coriander, turmeric, mustard seed, chili flakes, and oil. Season generously with salt and pepper.

2 Cut the chicken into finger-width strips. Place in a large bowl and toss with the spices. Leave to marinate at least 2 hours, or as long as possible.

3 Cook the chicken in a preheated oven, 425°F, 15 minutes, turning once or twice.

4 ▲ Meanwhile, make the yogurt chutney. Process the yogurt and herbs in a food processor until smooth, or finely chop the herbs and stir into the yogurt. Add the lime juice and season well with salt and pepper. Place the yogurt chutney in a small bowl and garnish with a sprig of parsley.

5 ▼ To serve, split the pita breads and warm them through. Stuff generously with salad greens, cucumber slices, and tomatoes. Divide the chicken strips between the breads. Spoon a little yogurt chutney over and serve.

SUPER CLUB SANDWICH

Club sandwiches are intended to be adequate substitutes for a light meal and can be as many layers high as you can manage!

SERVES 1

INGREDIENTS:
3 slices white or wholemeal bread
4 tbsp butter
1 cup shredded cooked skinless, boneless chicken
3 tbsp lemon mayonnaise
4 small crisp lettuce leaves
1 tomato, sliced
2-inch piece cucumber, sliced
salt and pepper

TO GARNISH:
sprigs of watercress
lemon wedges

1 Toast the white or wholemeal bread until golden. Spread each slice of toast with butter.

2 ▲ In a small bowl, mix the chicken with the mayonnaise. Add salt and pepper to taste.

3 Cover the first slice of toast with two of the lettuce leaves, then half of the chicken mixture and all of the tomato slices.

4 ▲ Top with the second slice of toast. Add the remaining chicken mixture and all the cucumber slices.

5 Place the third slice of toast on top, buttered side down, and press gently to seal.

6 ▼ With a sharp knife, cut the whole club sandwich into quarters or two large triangles. Secure each sandwich with a toothpick for easier eating. Serve the sandwiches garnished with a sprig of watercress and a lemon wedge.

SPICED CHICKEN KOFTAS

Koftas are spicy balls of ground poultry or meat. Lime pickle, a spicy Indian condiment, is available in Asian food stores.

SERVES 4

INGREDIENTS:
3 cups coarsely chopped skinless, boneless chicken
1 garlic clove
1-inch piece fresh gingerroot, grated
1/2 green bell pepper, seeded and chopped coarsely
2 fresh green chilies, seeded and chopped
4 tsp garam masala or curry powder
1/2 tsp ground turmeric
2 tbsp chopped fresh cilantro
1/2 tsp salt
6 tbsp vegetable oil
lime pickle, to serve

TO GARNISH:
sprigs of cilantro
lime wedges

1 Put all the ingredients, except the oil and lime pickle, into a food processor or blender and process until the mixture is finely chopped. Alternatively, chop the chicken, garlic, ginger, bell pepper, and chilies very finely. Mix together in a bowl with the garam masala, turmeric, cilantro and salt.

2 ▲ Using your hands, shape the mixture into 16 small balls.

3 ▼ Heat the oil in a wok or large skillet. Add the koftas and fry 8 to 10 minutes, turning occasionally. Fry in batches if necessary, keeping the first batch warm in a low oven.

4 ▲ Drain the koftas on paper towels. Serve hot with lime pickle.

THAI CHICKEN EGG ROLLS

A cucumber dipping sauce tastes perfect with these delicious Thai egg rolls, which are filled with stir-fried chicken and fresh, crunchy vegetables.

SERVES 4

INGREDIENTS:
1 tbsp light soy sauce
1 tsp sugar
2 tsp cornstarch, blended with 2 tbsp cold water
2 tbsp vegetable oil
4 scallions, trimmed and very finely sliced
1 carrot, cut into matchstick pieces
1 small green or red bell pepper, seeded and finely sliced
⅔ cup sliced button mushrooms
1 cup bean sprouts
1 cup shredded cooked skinless, boneless chicken
12 8-inch egg roll or won-ton wrappers
vegetable oil for deep-frying
salt and pepper
scallion brushes, to garnish

DIPPING SAUCE:
¼ cup malt or distilled vinegar
2 tbsp water
¼ cup light brown sugar
½ tsp salt
2-inch piece of cucumber, peeled and finely chopped
4 scallions, trimmed and finely sliced
1 small red or green chili, seeded and very finely chopped

1 Mix together the soy sauce, sugar, and cornstarch paste.

2 Heat the oil in a wok or skillet until it is very hot. Add the scallions, carrot, and bell pepper. Stir-fry 2 to 3 minutes. Add the mushrooms, bean sprouts, and chicken and stir-fry 2 minutes longer. Season with salt and pepper.

3 Add the cornstarch mixture to the stir-fry and cook, stirring continuously, about 1 minute, until thickened. Leave to cool.

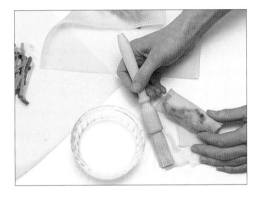

4 ▲ Place spoonfuls of the chicken mixture on to the egg roll wrappers. Dampen the edges and roll them up to enclose the filling completely.

5 ▲ To make the dipping sauce, heat the vinegar, water, sugar, and salt in a saucepan. Boil 1 minute. Mix the cucumber, scallions, and chili together in a small serving bowl. Pour the vinegar mixture over. Leave to cool.

6 Heat the oil and deep-fry the egg rolls until crisp and golden brown. Drain on paper towels. Serve, garnished with scallion brushes and accompanied by the cucumber dipping sauce.

CHICKEN "SCALLOPS"

Served in scallop shells, this dish makes a stylish presentation for a dinner-party first course.

SERVES 4

INGREDIENTS:

1½ cups short-cut macaroni, or other
   short dried pasta shapes
3 tbsp vegetable oil, plus extra for
   brushing
1 onion, finely chopped
3 slices bacon, chopped
1½ cups thinly sliced button
   mushrooms
¾ cup diced cooked skinless, boneless
   chicken,
¾ cup crème fraîche or sour cream
4 tbsp dry bread crumbs
½ cup sharp cheddar, grated
salt and pepper
sprigs of flat-leafed parsley,
   to garnish

1 Cook the macaroni or other pasta in a large pan of boiling salted water with 1 tablespoon of the oil. When the pasta is almost tender, drain it in a colander, return to the pan, and cover to keep warm.

2 ▲ Heat the remaining oil in a pan over medium heat. Add the onion and fry until it is translucent. Add the chopped bacon and mushrooms and cook 3 to 4 minutes longer, stirring once or twice.

3 Stir in the pasta, chicken, and the crème fraîche and season to taste.

4 ▲ Brush four large scallop shells with oil. Spoon in the chicken mixture and smooth to make neat mounds.

5 ▼ Mix together the bread crumbs and cheese. Sprinkle over the top of the chicken mixture. Press the topping lightly into the chicken. Place under a heated medium broiler 4 to 5 minutes until golden brown and bubbling. Garnish with parsley sprigs and serve hot.

SOUPS

*Laden with flavor and aroma, soup made with chicken
must be the most comforting dish in the world. It produces a
definite feeling of well-being which can help lift fatigue,
and it's easy to digest but still satisfying. Chicken soup
has long been heralded as a cure for countless illnesses.
For the best results, choose a stewing chicken or large
roaster; young birds sold for frying have not yet developed
the richness of flavor necessary for a satisfying soup.
Most chicken soups benefit from a good-quality
homemade stock, although the better brands of bouillon
cubes are adequate substitutes. Every cuisine in the world
has its favorite chicken soup recipe. In this chapter
you'll find a selection from places as far afield as China,
Mexico, and Scotland. They are all delicious and easy
to make, and will be successful every time.*

CHICKEN & GARBANZO BEAN SOUP (PAGE 26)

CHICKEN & CORN SOUP

A hint of chili and sherry flavor this tasty chicken and corn soup, which combines both baby corn cobs and corn kernels with red bell pepper and tomato to add color and flavor.

SERVES 4

INGREDIENTS:
1 skinless, boneless chicken breast half, about 6 ounces
2 tbsp sunflower oil
2 to 3 scallions, thinly sliced diagonally
1 small or ¹/₂ large red bell pepper, cored, seeded, and thinly sliced
1 garlic clove, crushed
4 ounces baby corn cobs, thinly sliced
4¹/₂ cups chicken stock
1 can (7-ounce) of whole-kernel corn, well drained
2 tbsp sherry
2 to 3 tsp bottled sweet chili sauce
2 to 3 tsp cornstarch
2 tomatoes, quartered, seeded, and sliced
salt and pepper
chopped fresh cilantro or parsley, to garnish

1 ▼ Cut the chicken meat into four strips lengthwise. Cut each strip into narrow slices across the grain.

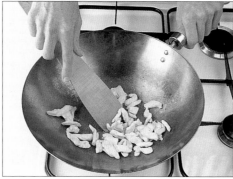

2 ▲ Heat the oil in a wok or large skillet, swirling it around until it is really hot. Add the chicken and stir-fry 3 to 4 minutes, stirring it around the wok until it is sealed all over and almost cooked through.

3 Add the scallions, bell pepper, and garlic to the wok or skillet. Continue stir-frying 2 to 3 minutes. Add the baby corn cobs and chicken stock. Bring to a boil.

4 ▼ Add the corn kernels, sherry, sweet chili sauce ,and salt to taste. Simmer 5 minutes, stirring from time to time.

5 Blend the cornstarch with a little cold water. Add to the soup and return to a boil. Add the tomato slices, adjust the seasoning, and simmer for a few minutes longer. Serve the soup very hot, sprinkled with finely chopped cilantro or parsley.

CHICKEN SOUP WITH ALMONDS

This soup can also be made using turkey or pheasant breasts. Pheasant gives a stronger, gamy flavor, particularly if game stock is made from the carcass and used in the soup.

SERVES 4

INGREDIENTS:
*1 large or 2 small skinless, boneless
    chicken breast halves
1 tbsp sunflower oil
1 carrot, cut into julienne strips
4 scallions, thinly sliced
    diagonally
3 cups chicken stock
finely grated peel of ¹/₂ lemon
¹/₃ cup blanched almonds, finely
    ground
1 tbsp light soy sauce
1 tbsp lemon juice
¹/₄ cup slivered almonds, toasted
salt and pepper
crusty bread, to serve*

1 Cut each piece of chicken into four strips lengthwise. Very thinly slice across the grain into shreds.

2 ▲ Heat the oil in a wok, swirling it around until really hot. Add the chicken and stir-fry 3 to 4 minutes until sealed and almost cooked through. Add the carrot and continue stir-frying 2 to 3 minutes, stirring all the time. Add the scallions and stir together.

3 ▲ Add the stock to the wok and bring to a boil. Add the lemon peel, ground almonds, soy sauce, and lemon juice. Season with salt and pepper.

4 Return to a boil. Lower the heat and simmer, uncovered, 5 minutes, stirring from time to time.

5 Adjust the seasoning to taste. Add most of the toasted slivered almonds and continue to cook the soup 1 to 2 minutes longer.

6 Serve the soup very hot, in individual bowls, sprinkled with the remaining almonds.

CHICKEN & GARBANZO BEAN SOUP

A good tasty soup full of vegetables, chicken and garbanzo beans, with just a hint of spiciness, to serve on any occasion.

SERVES 4 TO 6

INGREDIENTS:
3 tbsp olive oil
1 large onion, finely chopped
2 to 3 garlic cloves, crushed
½ to 1 red chili, seeded and very finely chopped
1 skinless, boneless chicken breast half, about 5 ounces, thickly sliced
2 celery stalks, finely chopped
1¼ cups coarsely grated carrots
2 bay leaves
6¼ cups chicken stock
½ tsp dried oregano
¼ tsp ground cinnamon
1 can (14-ounce) garbanzo beans, drained
1½ cups tomatoes, peeled, seeded, and chopped
1 tbsp tomato paste
salt and pepper
chopped fresh cilantro or parsley, to garnish
corn or wheat tortillas, to serve

1 Heat the oil in a large saucepan. Add the onion, garlic and chili, and fry very gently until softened but not colored.

2 ▲ Add the chicken slices to the saucepan and continue cooking until well sealed.

3 ▲ Add the celery, carrots, bay leaves, stock, oregano, cinnamon, salt, and pepper. Bring to a boil. Cover and simmer about 20 minutes, or until the chicken is tender.

4 ▼ Remove the chicken from the soup and cut it into narrow strips or chop it finely.

5 Return the chicken to the pan with the garbanzo beans, tomatoes and tomato paste. Simmer, covered, 15 to 20 minutes longer. Discard the bay leaves, then adjust the seasoning.

6 Serve very hot sprinkled with cilantro or parsley and accompanied by warmed tortillas.

COCK-A-LEEKIE SOUP

A traditional soup from Scotland in which a whole chicken is cooked with vegetables to add extra flavor to the broth. Add some of the cooked chicken to the soup and reserve the remainder for another meal.

SERVES 4 TO 6

INGREDIENTS:
2- to 3-pound chicken, including giblets, if available
8 to 9 cups chicken stock
1 onion, thinly sliced
4 leeks, thinly sliced
good pinch of ground allspice or ground coriander seeds
1 bouquet garni (bay leaf, parsley, and thyme sprigs, tied with string)
12 prunes, halved and stoned
salt and pepper
warm crusty bread, to serve

1 ▽ Put the chicken, giblets if using, stock and onion in a large saucepan. Bring to a boil and remove any gray foam from the surface using a draining spoon.

2 ▽ Add the leeks, allspice or coriander, bouquet garni, salt, and pepper. Cover and simmer 1½ hours until the chicken is cooked through and falling off the bone.

3 Remove the chicken from the pan and skim any fat from the surface of the soup.

4 ▲ Chop some of the chicken flesh and return to the pan. Add the prunes. Bring back to a boil, and simmer, uncovered, about 20 minutes.

5 Discard the bouquet garni. Adjust the seasoning and serve.

CHICKEN & CHESTNUT SOUP

A rich soup made from a full-flavored stock with pieces of chicken and chopped chestnuts for an interesting flavor and texture.

SERVES 4 TO 6

INGREDIENTS:
2 onions
1 raw or cooked chicken carcass, chopped, plus trimmings
chicken giblets, if available
6¼ cups water
1 bouquet garni (bay leaf, parsley, and thyme sprigs, tied with string)
4 ounces fresh chestnuts, pierced and roasted about 5 minutes, or boiled 30 to 40 minutes and drained, or 6 ounces canned peeled chestnuts
3 tbsp butter or margarine
⅓ cup all-purpose flour
⅔ cup milk
½ tsp ground coriander seeds
1½ cups coarsely grated carrots
1 tbsp chopped fresh parsley (optional)
salt and pepper

1 ▼ Cut one of the onions into quarters. Put the chicken carcass, giblets if available, water, the quartered onion, and the bouquet garni into a saucepan. Bring to a boil. Cover and simmer about 1 hour, stirring occasionally.

2 Strain the stock and reserve 4½ cups of liquid.

3 ▲ Remove the chicken trimmings from the carcass and finely chop ½ to ¾ cup. If using canned chestnuts, drain them well; if using fresh chestnuts, peel them. Finely chop the chestnuts. Chop the remaining onion.

4 Melt the butter or margarine in a saucepan. Add the onion and fry until soft. Stir in the flour and cook about 1 minute.

5 ▼ Gradually stir in the reserved stock and bring to a boil, stirring. Simmer 2 minutes. Add the milk, coriander, chopped chicken, carrots, chestnuts, salt, and pepper.

6 Bring the soup back to a boil. Simmer 10 minutes, then stir in the parsley, if using. Adjust the seasoning before serving.

CHICKEN & CORN CHOWDER

A quick and satisfying soup, full of flavor and different textures.

SERVES 2

INGREDIENTS:

2 tsp oil
1 tbsp butter or margarine
1 small onion, finely chopped
1 chicken quarter, halved, 1 leg, or
  2 to 3 drumsticks
1 tbsp all-purpose flour
2½ cups chicken stock
½ small red, yellow, or orange bell
  pepper, seeded and finely chopped
2 large tomatoes, peeled and chopped
2 tsp tomato paste
1 can (8-ounce) whole-kernel corn,
  drained
generous pinch of dried oregano
¼ tsp ground coriander seeds
salt and pepper
chopped fresh parsley, to garnish
crusty bread, to serve

1 ▼ Heat the oil and butter or margarine in a saucepan. Add the onion and fry until just beginning to soften. Add the chicken to the saucepan and fry until golden brown all over.

2 Stir in the flour and cook 1 to 2 minutes. Add the stock gradually. Bring to a boil and simmer about 5 minutes.

3 ▲ Add the bell pepper, chopped tomatoes, tomato paste, corn kernels, oregano, coriander, salt, and pepper. Cover and simmer gently about 20 minutes until the chicken is very tender.

4 ▲ Remove the chicken from the soup. Strip the flesh from the bone and chop it finely using a sharp knife. Return the chopped chicken to the soup.

5 Adjust the seasoning and simmer the soup 2 to 3 minutes longer before sprinkling with chopped fresh parsley. Serve the soup very hot with plenty of warm crusty bread.

NOODLES IN SOUP

Noodles in soup are popular in China. This is a thick, hearty soup. Add more stock if you prefer it thinner.

SERVES 4

INGREDIENTS:

8 ounces cooked, skinless, boneless
  chicken
3 or 4 Chinese dried mushrooms,
  soaked
1 can (4-ounce) sliced bamboo shoots,
  rinsed and drained
1½ cups shredded spinach, lettuce
  hearts, or Chinese leaves
2 scallions, finely shredded
8 ounces egg noodles
about 2½ cups chicken stock
2 tbsp light soy sauce
2 tbsp vegetable oil
1 tsp salt
½ tsp sugar
2 tsp Chinese rice wine or dry
  sherry
a few drops of sesame oil
1 tsp red chili oil (optional)

1 Cut the chicken into thin shreds. Squeeze dry the soaked mushrooms and discard the hard stem.

2 ▲ Thinly shred the Chinese dried mushrooms, bamboo shoots, spinach, and scallions.

3 Cook the noodles in boiling water following the directions on the package. Drain them and rinse under cold water. Place the noodles in a bowl; set aside.

4 Bring the stock to a boil. Add about 1 tablespoon of soy sauce and pour over the noodles. Keep warm.

5 ▲ Heat the oil in a heavy skillet. Add about half of the scallions, the chicken, mushrooms, bamboo shoots, and spinach. Stir-fry 2 to 3 minutes.

Add all the seasonings and blend together well.

6 ▼ Pour the mixture over the noodles. Garnish with the remaining scallions and serve.

HOT & SOUR SOUP

This is one of the most popular soups in Chinese restaurants throughout the world.

SERVES 4

INGREDIENTS:
*4 to 6 dried Chinese mushrooms,
   soaked
4 ounces cooked chicken or pork
1 cake tofu
2 ounces canned sliced bamboo shoots,
   drained
1 tbsp cornstarch
2½ cups chicken stock or water
1 tbsp Chinese rice wine or dry sherry
1 tbsp light soy sauce
2 tbsp rice vinegar
½ tsp ground white pepper
salt
2 or 3 scallions, thinly sliced,
   to garnish*

1 Drain the soaked Chinese mushrooms, squeeze them dry, and discard the hard stems. Thinly slice the mushrooms.

2 ▲ Using a cleaver, thinly slice the chicken, tofu and bamboo shoots into fine shreds; set aside.

3 Mix the cornstarch with 1½ tablespoons water to form a smooth paste; set aside.

4 ▼ Bring the chicken stock or water to a rolling boil in a wok or large skillet. Add the mushrooms, chicken, tofu, and bamboo shoots. Return to a boil and simmer about 1 minute.

5 ▲ Add the wine, soy sauce, and rice vinegar. Bring back to a boil, stirring in the cornstarch paste. Add the pepper and season with salt to taste. Serve hot, sprinkled with the sliced scallions.

CHICKEN & NOODLE ONE-POT

Flavorsome chicken and vegetables cooked with Chinese egg noodles in a coconut sauce. Increase the amount of stock if you prefer a thinner soup. Serve in deep soup bowls.

SERVES 4

INGREDIENTS:
1 tbsp sunflower oil
1 onion, sliced
1 garlic clove, crushed
1 inch fresh gingerroot, grated
1 bunch scallions, sliced
    diagonally
3 cups skinless, boneless chicken breasts
    cut into bite-sized pieces
2 tbsp mild curry paste
2 cups coconut milk
1¼ cups chicken stock
8 ounces Chinese egg noodles
2 tsp lime juice
salt and pepper
sprigs of basil, to garnish

1 Heat the oil in a wok or large, heavy-bottomed skillet. Add the onion, garlic, ginger, and scallions and stir-fry 2 minutes until softened.

2 ▲ Add the chicken pieces and curry paste. Stir-fry about 4 minutes until the vegetables and chicken are golden brown.

3 ▼ Stir in the coconut milk, stock, salt, and pepper to taste, stirring until well blended. Bring to a boil.

4 ▼ Break the noodles into large pieces, if necessary, and add to the pan. Cover and simmer 6 to 8 minutes, stirring occasionally, until the noodles are just tender.

5 Add the lime juice and adjust the seasoning. Garnish with sprigs of fresh basil. Serve at once in deep soup bowls.

LIGHT MEALS

A tasty but well-made light meal is the answer to today's hectic lifestyle. Family members may eat at different times, and many of us are too busy to prepare or eat a traditional three-course meal every day. Chicken is the perfect ingredient for a light meal. It's high in protein and B vitamins, and low in fat, so your diet will not suffer if you skip a full-scale meal now and then. Chicken can be cooked in countless ways and happily partners so many different flavors you'll find it difficult to run out of ideas. The selection in this chapter ranges from simple dishes such as Pasta Medley to the more unusual Bang-Bang Chicken from China. There are also some Mexican favorites such as Chicken Fajitas, as well as recipes for traditional chicken pies—delicious with a salad.

PASTA MEDLEY (PAGE 45)

SPICED CHICKEN & GRAPE SALAD

Tender chicken breasts, sweet grapes, and crisp celery are coated in a mild curry mayonnaise to make a wonderful al fresco lunch.

SERVES 4

INGREDIENTS:

*1 pound cooked skinless, boneless
  chicken breast
2 celery stalks, finely sliced
2 cups black grapes
$\frac{1}{2}$ cup slivered almonds, toasted
pinch of paprika
sprigs of fresh cilantro or flat-leafed
  parsley, to garnish*

CURRY SAUCE:

*$\frac{2}{3}$ cup mayonnaise
$\frac{1}{2}$ cup plain yogurt
1 tbsp clear honey
1 tbsp curry paste*

1 ▼ Cut the chicken into large pieces. Put in a bowl with the celery.

2 ▼ Halve the grapes and remove the seeds. Add to the chicken and celery.

3 ▼ To make the curry sauce, mix the mayonnaise, yogurt, honey, and curry paste together until blended.

4 ▲ Pour the curry sauce over the salad. Toss together carefully until all the ingredients are coated.

5 Transfer to a shallow serving dish and sprinkle with the almonds and paprika. Garnish with the cilantro or parsley.

CHICKEN WITH LEMON & TARRAGON

Boneless chicken breasts are cooked with saffron, white wine, and stock flavored with lemon peel and tarragon. The sauce is then thickened with egg yolks and sour cream and finished with mayonnaise.

SERVES 6

INGREDIENTS:
*6 large skinless, boneless chicken
  breast halves*
¼ tsp saffron strands
1 cup boiling water
1 tbsp olive oil
2 tbsp butter
1 garlic clove, crushed
½ cup dry white wine
grated peel of 1 small lemon
1 tbsp lemon juice
1 to 2 tbsp chopped fresh tarragon
2 tsp cornstarch
1 egg yolk
6 tbsp sour cream or heavy cream
4 tbsp mayonnaise
salt and pepper

TO GARNISH:
sprigs of fresh tarragon
lemon twists

1 ▼ Using a sharp knife, cut each of the chicken breast halves almost horizontally into three thin slices. Season each piece well with salt and pepper.

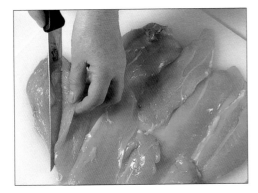

2 Put the saffron strands into a heatproof bowl. Pour in the boiling water and leave to stand until needed.

3 Heat the oil, butter, and garlic in a skillet. When foaming, add the chicken and fry on each side until lightly colored.

4 ▲ Add the saffron liquid, wine, half the tarragon, and the lemon peel and juice. Bring to a boil. Simmer about 5 minutes, or until tender.

5 Remove the chicken pieces with a draining spoon and place on a serving dish in overlapping slices. Leave to cool. Meanwhile, boil the remaining juices in the pan 3 to 4 minutes to reduce slightly.

6 Blend the cornstarch, egg yolk, and cream together in a bowl. Whisk in a little of the cooking juices, then return to the pan and heat gently, stirring continuously, until thickened and just barely simmering. Remove from the heat, adjust the seasoning, and pour into a bowl. Cover and leave until cool.

7 ▼ Beat the mayonnaise and remaining fresh tarragon into the sauce. Spoon over the chicken. Cover and chill thoroughly. Garnish with sprigs of fresh tarragon and lemon twists when ready to serve.

BANG-BANG CHICKEN

The cooked chicken meat is tenderized by being pounded with a rolling pin – hence the name of this very popular dish from Szechuan in China.

SERVES 4

INGREDIENTS:
4½ cups water
2 chicken quarters
1 cucumber, cut into matchstick
   shreds

SAUCE:
2 tbsp light soy sauce
1 tsp sugar
1 tbsp finely chopped scallion
1 tsp red chili oil
¼ tsp pepper
1 tsp white sesame seeds
2 tbsp peanut butter, creamed with a
   little sesame oil

1 ▼ Bring the water to a rolling boil in a large saucepan or a wok. Add the chicken pieces, reduce the heat, cover, and simmer 30 to 35 minutes.

2 ▼ Remove the chicken from the pan and immerse it in a bowl of cold water at least 1 hour to cool it, ready for shredding.

3 Remove the chicken pieces with a draining spoon and drain well. Pat dry with paper towels. Strip all the meat from the bone.

4 ▲ On a flat surface, using a rolling pin, pound the chicken to flatten. Tear the meat into shreds with two forks. Mix with the shredded cucumber and arrange in a serving dish.

5 To serve, mix together all the sauce ingredients. Pour over the chicken and cucumber.

THAI-STYLE CHICKEN-FRIED RICE

A few authentic ingredients give this spicy fried rice and chicken dish a typically Thai flavor.

SERVES 4

INGREDIENTS:
1¼ cups white long-grain rice
4 tbsp vegetable oil
2 garlic cloves, finely chopped
6 shallots, finely sliced
1 red bell pepper, seeded and diced
1 cup green beans, cut into 1-inch
 pieces
1 tbsp Thai red curry paste
2½ cups chopped cooked skinless,
 boneless chicken
½ tsp ground coriander seeds
1 tsp finely grated fresh
 gingerroot
2 tbsp Thai fish sauce
finely grated peel of 1 lime
3 tbsp lime juice
1 tbsp chopped fresh cilantro
salt and pepper

TO GARNISH:
lime wedges
sprigs of fresh cilantro

1 Cook the rice in boiling, lightly salted water 12 to 15 minutes until tender. Drain, rinse in cold water, and drain again thoroughly.

2 ▼ Heat the oil in a large skillet or wok. Add the garlic and shallots and fry gently for 2 to 3 minutes until golden.

3 ▼ Add the red bell pepper and green beans and stir-fry 2 minutes. Add the Thai curry paste and stir-fry 1 minute longer.

4 ▲ Add the cooked rice to the pan with the chicken, ground coriander seeds, ginger, Thai fish sauce, lime peel and juice, and fresh cilantro. Stir-fry over a medium-high heat 4 to 5 minutes until the rice and chicken are thoroughly reheated. Season to taste.

5 Garnish with lime wedges and cilantro before serving.

CRUNCHY-TOPPED CHICKEN/SPICED CHICKEN SALAD

Cook four chicken pieces together, and serve two hot, topped with a crunchy herb mixture and white sauce, accompanied by potatoes or pasta. Then mix the remaining ingredients with grapes and a delicious curry sauce to make a spicy chicken salad.

SERVES 2

INGREDIENTS:
4 chicken thighs
oil for brushing
garlic powder
1/2 eating apple, coarsely grated
1 1/2 tbsp packaged parsley and thyme
  stuffing mix
salt and pepper
cooked pasta shapes, to serve

SAUCE:
1 tbsp butter or margarine
2 tsp all-purpose flour
5 tbsp milk
2 tbsp dry white wine or stock
1/2 tsp dried mustard powder
1 tsp capers or chopped
  gherkins
salt and pepper

SPICED CHICKEN SALAD:
1/2 small onion, finely chopped
1 tbsp oil
1 tsp tomato paste
1/2 tsp curry powder
1 tsp apricot jam
1 tsp lemon juice
2 tbsp mayonnaise
1 tbsp sour cream or plain yogurt
3/4 cup seedless grapes, halved
salt and pepper
1/4 cup white long-grain rice, cooked,
  to serve

1 Place all four chicken thighs in a shallow baking dish. Brush with oil, sprinkle with garlic powder, and season with salt and pepper. Bake in a preheated oven, 400°F, 25 minutes, or until almost cooked through.

2 ▼ Combine the apple with the stuffing mixture. Baste the chicken, then spoon the mixture over two of the pieces. Return all the chicken pieces to the oven about 10 minutes longer, or until the chicken is cooked through.

3 To make the sauce, melt the butter or margarine in a pan. Stir in the flour and cook 1 to 2 minutes. Add the milk gradually, then the wine or stock, and bring to a boil. Stir in the mustard, capers or gherkins, and seasoning to taste. Simmer 1 minute. Serve the two crunchy-topped pieces of chicken with the sauce and pasta shapes.

4 For the salad, fry the onion gently in the oil until lightly colored. Add the tomato paste, curry powder, and jam. Cook 1 minute. Leave the mixture to cool.

5 Blend the mixture in a food processor, or press through a strainer. Beat in the lemon juice, mayonnaise, and sour cream or yogurt. Season to taste with salt and pepper.

6 ▼ Cut the chicken into strips. Add to the sauce with the grapes and stir together. Chill for at least 2 hours. Serve with the rice.

CHICKEN & HAM PIE

Made with a yogurt-based piecrust dough, this pie has a really moist filling and a melt-in-the-mouth crust.

SERVES 6

🍄🍄🍄🍄🍄🍄🍄🍄🍄🍄🍄🍄🍄🍄

INGREDIENTS:
4 tbsp butter
¼ cup all-purpose flour
⅔ cup milk
⅔ cup plain yogurt
2 small leeks, sliced
1½ cups finely diced skinless, boneless chicken breasts
1½ cups diced cooked ham
1 tsp soy sauce
pepper
dill sprigs, to garnish

PIECRUST:
2 cups all-purpose flour, plus extra for dusting
½ tsp mustard powder
¼ tsp salt
¾ cup butter, diced
about 3 tbsp plain yogurt
2 tbsp milk to glaze

🍄🍄🍄🍄🍄🍄🍄🍄🍄🍄🍄🍄🍄🍄

1 ▼ Grease a loose-bottomed tart pan, 1¾ inches deep. To make the piecrust, sift together the flour, mustard powder, and salt. Rub in the butter until the mixture resembles fine bread crumbs. Stir in enough yogurt to make a firm and nonsticky dough. Wrap the dough in foil and chill at least 30 minutes.

2 Melt 2 tablespoons of the butter in a pan over medium heat. Stir in the flour. Pour in the milk and yogurt, stirring all the time. Simmer, uncovered, 5 minutes. Remove from the heat, transfer the sauce to a bowl, and leave to cool.

3 Melt the remaining butter in a pan. Add the leeks and fry 2 to 3 minutes.

4 ▲ Pour the white sauce over the leeks. Add the chicken and ham and cook 5 minutes. Add the soy sauce and season with pepper. Remove from the heat and let cool completely.

5 ▲ Roll out the dough on a floured board. Use just over half of the dough to line the greased pan. Pour in the cold filling. Roll out the remaining dough and cover the pie. Trim the edges and press together firmly. Brush the top with milk. Re-roll the trimmings and cut into decorative shapes. Arrange the shapes over the pie and brush with milk. Bake in a preheated oven, 400°F, 35 minutes, or until golden brown. Serve the pie hot or cold.

RAISED CHICKEN PIE

A filling of diced chicken leg meat, ground pork, and bacon with pickled walnuts, mushrooms, and herbs is enclosed in a hot-water-pastry crust.

SERVES 6

INGREDIENTS:
12 ounces skinless, boneless chicken thighs
4 ounces lean ground pork
4 ounces cooked ham, coarsely ground or finely chopped
1 small onion, very finely chopped
2/3 cup roughly chopped button mushrooms
1 tbsp chopped fresh parsley
good pinch of ground coriander seeds
6 pickled walnuts, well drained
beaten egg or milk, to glaze
1 tsp unflavoured gelatin
2/3 cup chicken stock
salt and pepper

PIECRUST:
3 cups all-purpose flour
1 tsp salt
1/3 cup shortening
6 tbsp water
3 tbsp milk

1 To make the filling, chop the chicken thighs and mix with the pork, ham, onion, mushrooms, parsley, ground coriander, salt, and pepper.

2 To make the piecrust, sift the flour and salt into a bowl. Put the shortening in a saucepan with the water and milk and heat until melted. Bring to a boil. Pour onto the flour and mix until a smooth dough is formed.

3 Roll out about three-quarters of the dough, and use to line a lightly greased raised pie mold or a loaf pan.

4 ▲ Spoon half the chicken mixture into the lined pan. Arrange the walnuts on top. Cover with the remaining chicken mixture. Roll out the reserved dough for a lid, dampen the edges, and position. Trim and crimp the edge. Make a hole in the middle for steam to escape during baking. Garnish with dough leaves and glaze with beaten egg or milk.

5 Bake on a cookie sheet in a preheated oven, 400°F, 30 minutes. Reduce the temperature to 350°F,

glaze again, and bake 1 hour longer. When browned, cover with a sheet of baking parchment. Remove the pie from the oven and leave to cool for 10 minutes.

6 ▼ Dissolve the gelatin in the chicken stock, bringing just to a boil, and season well. Gradually pour in as much stock as possible through the hole in the pastry lid. Leave until cool, then chill thoroughly for at least 12 hours. Unmold the pie before serving.

THREE MEAT PACKAGE

Boneless pieces of chicken, lamb, and pork are layered with sage leaves, wrapped in spinach leaves, covered with a layer of cottage cheese, and enclosed in puff pastry. Delicious served cold and cut into slices.

SERVES 8

INGREDIENTS:
10 to 12 ounces pork tenderloin
about 12 fresh sage leaves
8 to 10 ounces lamb neck tenderloin
2 skinless, boneless chicken breast halves, total weight about 10 ounces
2 tbsp oil
4 ounces large spinach leaves
12 ounces store-bought puff pastry dough, thawed if frozen
1 cup cottage cheese
pinch of ground allspice
pinch of garlic powder
beaten egg or milk to glaze
salt and pepper

TO GARNISH:
sprigs of sage
cucumber slices

1 ▼ Layer the meat, beginning with the pork tenderloin. Cover with half the sage leaves, then add the lamb tenderloin, the rest of the sage leaves, and finally the chicken. Secure with fine string and/or skewers.

2 Heat the oil in a skillet. Add the layered meats and fry about 15 minutes, turning, until browned and partly cooked. Remove from the skillet and leave until cold.

3 Blanch the spinach leaves in boiling water for 2 minutes. Rinse in cold water and drain thoroughly.

4 ▼ Roll out the dough thinly into a rectangle large enough to enclose the layered meats and allow for five narrow strips to be cut off the edge. Cut off the strips. Lay the spinach down the middle of the dough and spread with the cottage cheese. Season well with allspice, garlic powder, salt, and pepper.

5 ▼ Remove the string or skewers from the meats and place the bundle on top of the cheese and spinach. Wrap up in the pastry, dampening the dough edges to secure. Place on a greased cookie sheet and glaze with beaten egg or milk. Lay the strips of pastry over the package and glaze again.

6 Bake the package in a preheated oven, 400°F, 30 minutes until the pastry is just beginning to brown. Reduce the temperature to 350°F and bake 20 minutes longer. Remove the package from the oven and leave to cool, then chill thoroughly in the refrigerator. Serve in slices, garnished with sage leaves and slices of cucumber.

CHICKEN & CORN PUFF

This delicious choux puff is an impressive dish yet it's simple to make. You can also use the choux pastry as a topping for all kinds of fillings.

SERVES 4

INGREDIENTS:
2 tbsp butter or margarine
¼ cup all-purpose flour
1¼ cups skim milk
1 cup shredded skinless, boneless cooked chicken
1 cup canned corn kernels, drained
1 tbsp chopped fresh parsley
salt and pepper

CHOUX PASTRY:
generous ½ cup all-purpose flour
4 tbsp butter or margarine
⅔ cup water
2 eggs, beaten
salt

1 ▼ To make the choux pastry, sift the flour and salt into a bowl. Put the butter or margarine and water into a pan and heat gently until the butter melts. Bring to a boil. Remove from the heat and add the flour all at once. Using a wooden spoon, beat until the mixture leaves the sides of the pan clean. Leave to cool slightly.

2 Gradually beat in the eggs until the mixture is thick and very glossy. Chill while making the filling.

3 To make the filling, put the butter or margarine, flour, and milk into a saucepan. Heat, whisking constantly, until smooth and thickened.

4 ▼ Add the chicken, corn, and parsley to the sauce. Season to taste with salt and pepper. Pour into a 1-quart shallow baking dish.

5 ▲ Spoon the choux pastry dough around the edge of the dish. Bake in a preheated oven, 425°F, 35 to 40 minutes until puffed up and golden brown. Serve at once.

TAGLIATELLE WITH CHICKEN & ALMONDS

Spinach tagliatelle covered with a rich tomato sauce and topped with creamy chicken makes an appetizing lunch or supper dish.

SERVES 4

INGREDIENTS:
4 tbsp unsalted butter
2¹/₂ cups thinly sliced skinless, boneless chicken breasts
³/₄ cup blanched almonds
1¹/₄ cups heavy cream
8 ounces fresh or dried green ribbon noodles
salt and pepper
basil leaves, to garnish

TOMATO SAUCE:
1 small onion, chopped
2 tbsp olive oil
1 garlic clove, chopped
1 can (14-ounce) crushed tomatoes
2 tbsp chopped fresh parsley
1 tsp dried oregano
2 bay leaves
2 tbsp tomato paste
1 tsp sugar

1 ▼ To make the tomato sauce, fry the onion gently in the oil until translucent. Add the garlic and fry 1 minute longer until just golden. Stir in the remaining ingredients and bring to a boil. Simmer, uncovered, 15 to 20 minutes until reduced by half. Discard the bay leaves; keep the sauce warm.

2 ▼ Melt the butter in a skillet. Add the chicken and almonds and fry 5 to 6 minutes, stirring frequently.

3 Meanwhile, put the cream in a small pan and boil about 10 minutes until reduced by almost half.

4 ▼ Stir the cream into the chicken mixture. Season with salt and pepper; set aside and keep warm.

5 Cook the pasta in a large pan of boiling salted water until just tender. Drain the pasta well, then put it in a warmed serving dish.

6 Spoon the tomato sauce over the pasta and top with the chicken mixture. Garnish with basil and serve.

CHICKEN-FILLED TORTELLINI

According to legend, tortellini are said to resemble Venus's belly button.

SERVES 4

INGREDIENTS:
1 cup chopped cooked skinless, boneless chicken breasts
2 ounces prosciutto
1½ ounces spinach, cooked and drained
1 tbsp finely chopped onion
2 tbsp grated Parmesan cheese
good pinch of ground allspice
1 egg, beaten
salt and pepper

PASTA DOUGH:
generous 2½ cups all-purpose flour
pinch of salt
3 large eggs
1 tbsp olive oil
1 tbsp water

SAUCE:
1¼ cups light cream
1 or 2 garlic cloves, crushed
2 cups thinly sliced mushrooms
4 tbsp freshly grated Parmesan cheese
1 to 2 tbsp freshly chopped parsley
salt and pepper

1 ▲ To make the pasta dough, sift the flour and salt onto a flat surface. Make a well in the middle. Beat the eggs, oil, and water together, and pour into the well. Work in the flour to form a dough. Knead 10 to 15 minutes until smooth. Cover with a damp cloth and let rest for 10 to 15 minutes.

2 To make the filling, put the chicken into a food processor with the prosciutto, spinach, and onion. Process until finely chopped. Add the Parmesan, allspice, seasonings, and egg.

3 ▲ Roll out the dough, half at a time, as thinly as possible. Cut into 1½- to 2-inch circles. Place ½ teaspoon filling on each circle. Fold into a semicircle, sealing the edges firmly. Wrap a semicircle round your index finger, crossing the ends. Press firmly together. Curl the rest of the dough back to make a "belly button" shape. Remove from your finger and put on a floured tray. Repeat with the rest of the dough, re-rolling the trimmings.

4 ▼ Bring a large pan of salted water to a boil. Add the tortellini in batches. Once they rise to the surface, cook about 5 minutes, giving an occasional stir. Remove with a draining spoon and drain on paper towels. Keep warm in a serving dish while cooking the remainder.

5 To make the sauce, heat the cream with the garlic and bring to a boil. Simmer a few minutes. Add the mushrooms, half the Parmesan, and seasoning and simmer 2 to 3 minutes longer. Stir in the parsley. Pour over the warm tortellini. Sprinkle with the remaining Parmesan and serve immediately.

PASTA MEDLEY

Strips of cooked chicken are tossed with colored pasta, grapes, and carrot sticks in a pesto-flavored dressing. Any leftovers keep well in the refrigerator a day or two.

SERVES 2

INGREDIENTS:
4 to 5 ounces dried pasta shapes, such
  as twists or bows
1 tbsp oil
2 tbsp mayonnaise
2 tsp bottled pesto sauce
1 tbsp sour cream or plain yogurt
6 ounces cooked skinless; boneless
  chicken meat
1 or 2 celery stalks
1 cup black grapes (preferably
  seedless)
1 large carrot, trimmed
salt and pepper
celery leaves, to garnish

FRENCH DRESSING:
1 tbsp wine vinegar
3 tbsp extra-virgin olive oil
salt and pepper

1 To make the French dressing, whisk all the dressing ingredients together until smooth.

2 ▼ Cook the pasta with the oil in plenty of boiling salted water about 12 minutes until just tender. Drain thoroughly, rinse, and drain again. Transfer to a bowl and stir in 1 tablespoon of the French dressing while hot; leave until cold.

3 Combine the mayonnaise, pesto sauce, and sour cream or yogurt in a bowl. Season to taste.

4 ▲ Cut the chicken into thin strips. Cut the celery stalks diagonally into thin slices. Reserve a few of the grapes for garnish, halve the rest, and remove any seeds. Cut the carrot into thin strips.

5 ▼ Add the chicken, celery, halved grapes, carrot, and mayonnaise mixture to the cold pasta. Toss together thoroughly. Check the seasoning and add more salt and pepper if necessary.

6 Arrange the pasta mixture on two plates and garnish with the reserved black grapes and the celery leaves.

CHICKEN FAJITAS

This spicy chicken filling, made with mixed bell peppers, chilies, and mushrooms is strongly flavored with lime. It is served in folded tortillas and topped with sour cream, sliced red onion, chopped tomato, and lime wedges. Other ingredients can also be mixed with the chicken—the possibilities are endless.

SERVES 4

INGREDIENTS:
2 red bell peppers
2 green bell peppers
2 tbsp olive oil
2 onions, chopped
3 garlic cloves, crushed
1 chili, seeded and finely chopped
2 skinless, boneless chicken breast
  halves, about 12 ounces
1 cup sliced button mushrooms
2 tsp chopped fresh cilantro
grated peel of ¹/₂ lime
2 tbsp lime juice
4 wheat or corn tortillas
4 to 6 tbsp sour cream
salt and pepper

TO GARNISH:
sliced red onion
chopped tomatoes
lime wedges

1 ▼ Halve the red and green bell peppers, remove the seeds, and place skin-side up on a broiler pan. Broil until well charred. Leave to cool slightly, then peel off the skins. Cut the flesh into thin slices.

2 Heat the oil in a skillet. Add the onions, garlic, and chili, and fry for a few minutes until the onion softens.

3 ▲ Cut the chicken into thin strips. Add to the vegetable mixture in the skillet and fry 4 to 5 minutes until the chicken is almost cooked, stirring occasionally.

4 Add the bell peppers, mushrooms, cilantro, lime peel, and juice. Continue to cook 2 to 3 minutes. Season to taste.

5 ▲ Heat the tortillas, wrapped in foil, by placing in a preheated oven, 350°F, 4 to 5 minutes. Fold in half and divide the chicken mixture equally between them.

6 Top the chicken filling with sour cream. Serve garnished with red onion slices, chopped tomatoes, and lime wedges.

ENCHILADA LAYERS

You can vary the filling for these tasty layered Mexican tortillas by using beef, fish, or shellfish. If preferred, the filled tortillas can be rolled up, rather than being baked in layers.

SERVES 4

INGREDIENTS:
1 pound skinless, boneless chicken breast halves
2 tbsp olive oil
1 large onion, thinly sliced
3 garlic cloves, crushed
1 tsp ground cumin seeds
2 tbsp stock or water
1 tbsp chopped fresh cilantro
6 wheat or corn tortillas
1¹/₂ cups coarsely grated Feta cheese
salt and pepper
sprigs of fresh cilantro, to garnish

TOMATO SAUCE:
2 tbsp oil
1 onion, very finely chopped
3 garlic cloves, crushed
1 red chili, seeded and finely chopped
1 can (14-ounce) crushed tomatoes with herbs
1 can (8-ounce) peeled tomatoes, chopped
3 tbsp tomato paste
2 tbsp lime juice
2 tsp superfine sugar
salt and pepper

1 Chop the chicken breast meat finely. Heat the oil in a skillet. and fry the onion and garlic until softened.

2 ▲ Add the chicken and fry, stirring, about 5 minutes until well sealed and almost cooked through. Add the cumin, stock or water, salt, and pepper. Continue to cook 2 to 3 minutes until tender. Stir in the cilantro. Remove from the heat.

3 To make the tomato sauce, heat the oil in a pan. Add the onion, garlic, and chili and fry until softened.

4 Add both cans of tomatoes, the tomato paste, lime juice, sugar, and seasoning. Bring to a boil and simmer 10 minutes.

5 ▼ Place a tortilla on a greased ovenproof dish. Cover with one-fifth of the chicken mixture and 2 tablespoons of the tomato sauce. Sprinkle a layer of the grated cheese over. Continue layering, finishing with a tortilla and the remaining tomato sauce and cheese.

6 Place the enchiladas uncovered in a preheated oven, 375°F, and bake about 25 minutes, or until the top is lightly browned and bubbling. Serve the enchiladas cut into wedges and garnished with a sprig of cilantro.

CHICKEN BURRITOS

A filling of chopped chicken and scrambled eggs, together with sliced tomatoes and a spicy pumpkin seed, herb, and yogurt mixture, is rolled into wheat or corn tortillas.

SERVES 4

INGREDIENTS:

½ cup pumpkin seeds
3 or 4 scallions, trimmed and sliced
1 chili, seeded and finely chopped
4 tbsp chopped fresh flat-leafed parsley
1 tbsp chopped fresh cilantro
6 tbsp plain yogurt
4 wheat or corn tortillas
2 tbsp butter
4 tbsp milk
1 garlic clove, crushed
6 eggs, beaten lightly
1 cup shredded cooked skinless, boneless chicken
2 tomatoes, peeled and sliced
salt and pepper

TO GARNISH:
shredded lettuce
sliced red onions
chopped tomatoes

1 ▼ Toast the pumpkin seeds lightly in a heavy-bottomed skillet without any added fat. Put the toasted seeds into a food processor with the scallions and chili and work until well blended. Alternatively, chop the pumpkin seeds and scallions very finely and pound with the chili using a mortar and pestle.

2 ▲ Add the parsley, cilantro, and yogurt to the food processor. Blend until well mixed. Season to taste with salt and pepper.

3 Wrap the tortillas in foil and warm in a preheated oven, 350°F, 4 to 5 minutes.

4 Melt the butter with the milk, garlic, salt, and pepper. Remove from the heat and stir in the eggs. Cook over low heat, stirring, until just scrambled. Stir in the cooked chicken.

5 ▼ Lay the tortillas flat and spoon the scrambled egg down the middle of each tortilla. Top with the pumpkin seed mixture and the tomatoes.

6 Carefully roll up the tortillas. Serve garnished with the shredded lettuce, sliced red onions and chopped tomatoes.

SAUTÉS & STIR-FRIES

Tender and succulent, small cuts of chicken are perfect for sautéing and stir-frying. Both frying techniques are used throughout the world and are easy to master. They form the basis of a limitless number of dishes ranging from the classic Chicken Kiev to stir-fried Chinese Chicken with Noodles. The direct heat transmitted from the pan sears the surface of the meat and seals in the juices so the flesh retains moisture and flavor. If you're sautéing chicken with skin, cook the skin side thoroughly to render the fat and create a crispy texture. If you're stir-frying, cut the chicken into small, equal-sized cubes or strips so they cook evenly. Whichever method you choose, however, you can be sure of quickly cooked, mouthwatering meals every time.

CHICKEN, CILANTRO, GINGER & LEMON STIR-FRY (PAGE 54)

CHICKEN KIEV

This classic dish from the Ukraine is delicious served with sautéd potatoes.

SERVES 4

INGREDIENTS:
1 garlic clove, crushed
6 tbsp butter
4 skinless, boneless chicken breast halves
2 eggs, beaten
2 tbsp milk
vegetable oil for deep-frying
1 cup all-purpose flour
fresh bread crumbs, for coating
salt and pepper

TO GARNISH:
chopped parsley
lemon slices

1 ▼ Using a fork, mash the garlic into the butter. Season and shape into a square pattie. Chill in the freezer.

2 ▼ Slice each chicken breast half in half horizontally. Lay between sheets of plastic wrap and flatten to an even thickness. Cover and chill.

3 ▼ When the butter is firm, cut it into four batons. Place a baton lengthwise on four of the chicken pieces. Place another chicken piece on top. Cover and chill until ready to cook.

4 Beat the eggs and milk together. To cook the chicken Kiev, heat 2 inches oil to 375°F. Coat each Kiev with flour, then the egg and milk mixture, and finally the bread crumbs. Repeat the coating once more to form a good seal round the chicken. Fry each Kiev about 5 minutes. Serve immediately, accompanied by sautéd potatoes and garnished with chopped parsley and lemon slices.

SKILLET-COOKED CHICKEN & ARTICHOKES

Artichokes are a familiar ingredient in Italian cookery. In this dish, they are used as a delicate flavoring.

SERVES 4

INGREDIENTS:
4 chicken breast halves, part boned
2 tbsp olive oil
2 tbsp butter
2 red onions, cut into wedges
2 tbsp lemon juice
²/₃ cup dry white wine
²/₃ cup chicken stock
2 tsp all-purpose flour
1 can (14-ounce) artichokes, drained and halved
salt and pepper
chopped fresh parsley, to garnish

1 ▼ Season the chicken with salt and freshly ground black pepper. Heat the oil and 1 tablespoon butter in a large skillet. Add the chicken and fry 4 to 5 minutes on each side until lightly golden. Using a draining spoon, remove the chicken from the pan.

2 Toss the onion in the lemon juice. Add to the skillet and fry, stirring, 3 to 4 minutes until just beginning to soften.

3 ▼ Return the chicken to the skillet. Pour in the wine and chicken stock and bring to a boil. Cover and simmer 30 minutes.

4 Remove the chicken from the skillet, reserving the cooking juices. Transfer to a serving dish and keep warm. Bring the pan juices to a boil and boil rapidly 5 minutes.

5 Blend the remaining butter with the flour to form a paste. Reduce the heat and simmer the pan juices. Add the paste to the skillet, stirring until thickened.

6 ▼ Adjust the seasoning, stir in the artichokes, and cook 2 minutes longer. Pour over the chicken and garnish with parsley.

CHICKEN PAPRIKA

Paprika, caraway seeds, and sour cream give this dish an East European flavor. Paprika is a seasoning commonly used in Hungary.

SERVES 4

INGREDIENTS:
4 tbsp butter
4 chicken quarters
1 tbsp paprika
1 tbsp caraway seeds
1 onion, finely chopped
1 garlic clove, crushed
1 red bell pepper, finely chopped
1¹/₂ cups finely chopped mushrooms
4 ounces pancetta or smoked bacon, diced
¹/₃ cup sherry
²/₃ cup sour cream
1 tbsp cornstarch
salt and pepper

1 Melt the butter in a skillet. Add the chicken and brown on all sides. Stir in the paprika and caraway seeds and season. Transfer to a baking dish; set aside.

2 ▼ Add the onion and garlic to the skillet and fry slowly in the butter about 10 minutes.

3 Add the onion mixture to the chicken. Cover and bake in a preheated oven, 400°F, 40 minutes, turning once or twice. Remove the chicken and onions from the dish, reserving the cooking juices; set aside and keep warm.

4 ▼ Pour the cooking juices into a large skillet set over medium heat. Stir in the bell pepper, mushrooms, and pancetta or bacon, and fry for 15 minutes.

5 ▼ Add the sherry to the pan, and simmer to reduce. Season to taste with salt and pepper.

6 To finish the sauce, combine the sour cream and cornstarch. Stir into the pan until the sauce is smooth and thick. Adjust the seasoning to taste and serve the sauce with the chicken pieces.

CHICKEN & ALMOND RISSOLES WITH STIR-FRIED VEGETABLES

Cooked potatoes and cooked chicken are combined to make tasty rissoles rolled in chopped almonds. Serve with stir-fried vegetables.

SERVES 1

INGREDIENTS:

4 ounces peeled potatoes, boiled
3 ounces carrots
1 cup cooked chicken meat
1 garlic clove, crushed
1/2 tsp dried tarragon or thyme
generous pinch of ground allspice or ground coriander seeds
1 egg yolk or 1/2 egg, beaten
about 1/4 cup slivered almonds, finely chopped
salt and pepper

STIR-FRIED VEGETABLES:

1 celery stalk
2 scallions, trimmed
1 tbsp oil
8 baby corn cobs
about 10 to 12 snow peas or sugar-snap peas, trimmed
2 tsp balsamic vinegar
salt and pepper

1 ▼ Coarsely grate the boiled potatoes and raw carrots into a bowl. Finely chop or grind the chicken. Add to the vegetables with the garlic, tarragon or thyme, allspice or coriander, salt, and pepper.

2 Add the egg yolk or beaten egg to bind the ingredients together. Divide the mixture in half and shape into two large ovals.

3 ▼ Roll each rissole in the chopped almonds until evenly coated.

4 Place the rissoles in a greased baking dish. Bake in a preheated oven, 400°F, about 20 minutes, or until lightly browned. Alternatively, heat a little oil in a skillet and fry the rissoles until browned all over and cooked through.

5 ▲ While the rissoles bake, prepare the stir-fried vegetables. Cut the celery and scallions into thin, diagonal slices. Heat the oil in a skillet. Add the vegetables and stir-fry over high heat 1 to 2 minutes. Add the corn cobs and snowpeas and cook 2 to 3 minutes longer. Finally, stir in the balsamic vinegar and season with salt and pepper to taste.

6 Spoon the stir-fried vegetables onto a serving plate and serve the rissoles beside them. Serve at once.

CHICKEN, CILANTRO, GINGER & LEMON STIR-FRY

The pomegranate seeds add a pleasingly sharp Chinese flavor to this Asian-style stir-fry. The dish can also be served cold in the summer with a spicy rice salad or a mixed green salad.

SERVES 4

INGREDIENTS:

3 tbsp oil
4¹/₂ cups skinless, boneless chicken breasts cut into 2-inch strips
3 garlic cloves, crushed
1¹/₂-inch piece fresh gingerroot, cut into strips
1 tsp pomegranate seeds, crushed
¹/₂ tsp ground turmeric
1 tsp garam masala or curry powder
2 fresh green chilies, sliced
¹/₂ tsp salt
4 tbsp lemon juice
grated peel of 1 lemon
6 tbsp chopped fresh cilantro
¹/₂ cup chicken stock
naan bread, to serve

1 ▼ Heat the oil in a wok or large skillet. Add the chicken and stir-fry until golden brown all over. Remove from the pan; set aside.

2 Add the garlic, ginger, and pomegranate seeds to the wok. Stir-fry 1 minute, taking care not to let the garlic burn, or it will taste bitter.

3 ▼ Stir in the turmeric, garam masala, and chilies and stir-fry 30 seconds.

4 Return the chicken to the wok. Add the salt, lemon juice, lemon peel, cilantro, and chicken stock. Stir the chicken well to make sure it is coated in the sauce.

5 Bring the mixture to a boil. Lower the heat and simmer 10 to 15 minutes until the chicken is thoroughly cooked. Serve with warm naan bread.

CHICKEN WITH PEANUT SAUCE

A tangy stir-fry with a strong peanut flavor. Serve with freshly boiled rice or noodles.

SERVES 4

INGREDIENTS:

4 skinless, boneless chicken breast halves
4 tbsp soy sauce
4 tbsp sherry
3 tbsp crunchy peanut butter
12 ounces zucchini, trimmed
2 tbsp sunflower oil
4 to 6 scallions, thinly sliced diagonally
1 can (8-ounce) bamboo shoots, drained and sliced
salt and pepper
4 tbsp shredded coconut, toasted, to garnish

6 ▼ Add the peanut butter mixture and heat thoroughly, stirring all the time so everything is coated in the sauce as it thickens. Adjust the seasoning and serve very hot, sprinkled with the toasted coconut.

4 ▲ Heat the oil in a wok, swirling it around until it is really hot. Add the scallions and stir-fry 1 to 2 minutes. Add the chicken and stir-fry 3 to 4 minutes until well sealed and almost cooked.

5 Add the zucchini and bamboo shoots to the wok and continue stir-frying 1 to 2 minutes.

1 Cut the chicken into thin strips across the grain. Season lightly with salt and pepper.

2 Put the soy sauce in a bowl with the sherry and peanut butter. Stir until smooth and well blended.

3 ▲ Cut the zucchini into 2-inch pieces then cut into sticks about ¼ inch thick.

CHICKEN WITH MUSHROOMS

Use dried Chinese mushrooms for the best flavor in this dish.

SERVES 4

INGREDIENTS:

10 to 12 ounces skinless, boneless chicken thighs
1/2 tsp sugar
1 tbsp light soy sauce
1 tsp rice wine or dry sherry
2 tsp cornstarch
4 to 6 dried Chinese mushrooms, soaked in warm water and drained
1 tbsp finely shredded fresh gingerroot
a few drops of sesame oil
salt and pepper
cilantro leaves, to garnish

1 ▼ Cut the chicken into bite-sized pieces and place in a bowl. Stir in the sugar, soy sauce, wine or sherry, and cornstarch; leave to marinate 25 to 30 minutes.

2 ▼ Dry the mushrooms on paper towels. Slice into thin shreds, discarding any hard pieces of stem.

3 ▲ Place the chicken pieces on a heatproof dish that will fit inside a bamboo steamer. Arrange the mushroom and ginger shreds on top of the chicken. Sprinkle with sesame oil, salt, and pepper.

4 ▼ Place the dish on the rack inside a hot steamer or on a rack in a wok or large skillet filled with hot water. Steam over high heat 20 minutes. Serve immediately, garnished with cilantro leaves.

CHICKEN WITH BELL PEPPER

Red bell pepper or celery can also be used in this spicy Szechuan recipe — the method is the same.

SERVES 4

INGREDIENTS:
10 ounces skinless, boneless chicken
   breast halves
1 tsp salt
½ egg white
1 tsp cornstarch mixed to a paste with
   1½ tsp cold water
1 green bell pepper, seeded
1¼ cups vegetable oil
1 scallion, finely shredded
a few strips of fresh gingerroot, thinly
   shredded
1 or 2 red chilies, seeded and thinly
   shredded
½ tsp sugar
1 tbsp rice wine or dry sherry
a few drops of sesame oil

1 ▼ Cut the chicken breast halves into strips. Mix them in a bowl with a pinch of the salt, the egg white and the cornstarch paste, in that order.

2 Cut the bell pepper into thin shreds the same size and length as the chicken strips; set aside.

3 ▲ Heat the vegetable oil in a preheated wok or skillet to a temperature of 350 to 375°F, or until a cube of bread browns in 30 seconds. Deep-fry the chicken strips, in batches, for about 1 minute, or until the color changes and the strips are sealed. Remove with a draining spoon; set aside and keep warm.

4 ▼ Pour off the excess oil from the wok, leaving about 1 tablespoon. Add the scallion, ginger, chilies, and bell pepper. Stir-fry about 1 minute. Return the chicken to the wok together with the remaining salt, the sugar, and wine or sherry. Stir-fry 1 minute longer. Sprinkle with sesame oil and serve.

CHICKEN WITH CELERY & CASHEW NUTS

Yellow bean sauce gives this easy dish an authentic Chinese taste. Pecan nuts can be used in place of the cashews.

SERVES 4

INGREDIENTS:

3 or 4 skinless, boneless chicken breast halves, about 1¼ pounds
2 tbsp sunflower or vegetable oil
1 cup unsalted cashew nuts
4 to 6 scallions, thinly sliced diagonally
5 or 6 celery stalks, thinly sliced diagonally
¾ cup bottled yellow bean sauce
salt and pepper
boiled rice, to serve
celery leaves, to garnish (optional)

1 ▼ Cut the chicken into thin slices across the grain.

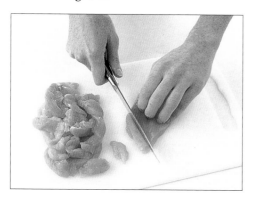

2 ▼ Heat the oil in a wok, swirling it around until hot. Add the cashew nuts and stir-fry until they begin to brown. Add the chicken and stir-fry until well sealed and almost cooked through.

3 ▲ Add the scallions and celery and continue stir-frying 2 to 3 minutes, stirring the ingredients constantly around the wok.

4 ▲ Stir in the yellow bean sauce. Season lightly with salt and pepper and toss until the chicken and vegetables are thoroughly coated with the sauce and are piping hot. Serve at once with plain boiled rice, garnished with celery leaves, if liked.

QUICK CHINESE CHICKEN WITH NOODLES

Chicken and fresh vegetables are flavored with ginger and Chinese five-spice powder in this quick-and-easy stir-fry. Vary your choice of vegetables according to what is in season. Make sure that the vegetables are as fresh as possible.

SERVES 4

INGREDIENTS:
6 ounces Chinese thread egg
  noodles
2 tbsp vegetable oil
1/4 cup shelled peanuts
1 bunch of scallions, sliced
1 green bell pepper, seeded and cut
  into thin strips
1 large carrot, cut into matchstick
  strips
4 ounces cauliflower, broken into
  small flowerettes
12 ounces skinless, boneless chicken,
  cut into strips
3 1/2 cups sliced mushrooms
1 tsp finely grated fresh gingerroot
1 tsp Chinese five-spice powder
1 tbsp chopped fresh cilantro
1 tbsp light soy sauce
salt and pepper
fresh chives, to garnish

1 Put the noodles into a large bowl and cover with boiling water. Leave to soak for 6 minutes, or according to the package directions.

2 ▲ Meanwhile, heat the vegetable oil in a preheated wok or large skillet. Add the peanuts and stir-fry about

1 minute until browned. Remove with a draining spoon and drain on paper towels.

3 ▲ Add the scallions, bell pepper, carrot, cauliflower, and chicken strips to the wok. Stir-fry over high heat 4 to 5 minutes until the chicken is cooked thoroughly. The vegetables should remain crisp and brightly colored.

4 ▼ Drain the soaked noodles thoroughly and add them to the wok. Add the mushrooms and stir-fry 2 minutes. Add the ginger, five-spice powder, and cilantro and stir-fry 1 minute longer.

5 Season with the soy sauce, salt, and pepper. Sprinkle with the peanuts. Garnish with chives and serve at once on warmed plates.

LIME & CILANTRO CHICKEN-FRIED RICE

Lime peel and juice are combined with fresh cilantro to give this dish a very lively Thai flavor.

SERVES 4

INGREDIENTS:
generous 1 cup long-grain white rice
4 tbsp vegetable oil
2 garlic cloves, finely chopped
1 small green chili, seeded and finely chopped
5 shallots, finely sliced
1 tbsp bottled Thai green curry paste
1 yellow or green bell pepper, seeded and chopped
2 celery stalks, finely sliced
1 1/2 cups chopped cooked skinless, boneless chicken
2 tbsp light soy sauce
finely grated peel of 1 lime
2 tbsp lime juice
1 tbsp chopped fresh cilantro
1/4 cup unsalted peanuts, toasted

TO GARNISH:
sprigs of fresh cilantro
finely sliced shallots
lime slices

1 Cook the rice in plenty of boiling, lightly salted water about 12 minutes until tender. Drain, rinse with cold water, and drain thoroughly again.

2 ▲ Heat the oil in a wok or large skillet. Add the garlic and fry slowly 2 minutes until golden. Add the chili and shallots and cook, stirring, 3 to 4 minutes longer until slightly softened.

3 ▲ Add the green curry paste to the wok and stir-fry 1 minute. Add the bell pepper and the celery and stir-fry over high heat 2 minutes until just softened.

4 ▲ Tip the cooked rice into the wok, stirring well. Add the chicken, soy sauce, lime peel and juice, and cilantro. Stir-fry over medium-high heat 4 to 5 minutes until the rice and chicken are heated.

5 Serve sprinkled with the toasted peanuts and garnished with sprigs of fresh cilantro, sliced shallots, and lime slices.

BROILS, GRILLS & ROASTS

*Few foods are more delicious than the juicy flesh
and slightly charred skin of a piece of chicken grilled
over an open fire. Lightly brushed with olive oil and
seasoned with coarsely ground black pepper, grilled or
broiled chicken is simplicity itself. Marinating the chicken
beforehand adds flavor and helps prevent the meat from
drying out during cooking. Use an Indian-style marinade
of yogurt and fragrant spices, or soy sauce, sesame, and
ginger for an Asian flavor, or try the Cajun-inspired marinade
in Blackened Chicken with Guacamole. Roasting is another
time-honored way of cooking chicken. Golden and
glistening, traditional roast chicken turns the simplest
meal into a celebration.*

CHICKEN SATAY KABOBS (PAGE 73)

STICKY CHICKEN WINGS

These need to be eaten with the fingers, so serve them at an informal supper.

SERVES 4 TO 6

INGREDIENTS:
1 small onion, finely chopped
2 garlic cloves, crushed
2 tbsp olive oil
2 cups puréed and sieved tomato
2 tsp dried thyme
1 tsp dried oregano
pinch of fennel seeds
3 tbsp red-wine vinegar
2 tbsp Dijon mustard
pinch of ground cinnamon
2 tbsp brown sugar
1 tsp chili flakes
2 tbsp black treacle
16 chicken wings
salt and pepper

1 ▼ Fry the onion and garlic in the oil about 10 minutes until soft.

2 ▼ Stir in the sieved tomatoes, thyme, oregano, fennel, red-wine vinegar, mustard, cinnamon, sugar,

chili flakes, treacle, salt, and pepper. Bring to a boil. Reduce the heat and simmer about 15 minutes, until slightly reduced.

3 ▲ Put the chicken wings in a large dish and coat liberally with the sauce. Marinade at least 3 hours, or as long as possible, stirring often.

4 ▼ Transfer the marinaded chicken wings to a foil-lined cookie sheet. Roast in a preheated oven, 425°F, 10 minutes. Reduce the heat to 375°F and roast 20 minutes longer, basting often.

5 Serve piping hot, garnished with celery stalks and cherry tomatoes.

LEMON & MINT CHICKEN BURGERS

Use chicken thigh or leg meat for these delicious burgers because it has much more flavor than breast meat.

SERVES 4

INGREDIENTS:
1½ pounds ground chicken leg meat
4 tbsp chopped fresh mint
grated peel of 1 lemon
4 tbsp lemon juice
olive oil
¾ cup stoned ripe olives, chopped
salt
lemon pepper (or black pepper)
1 round focaccia bread, plain or
  flavored
lettuce and lemon wedges, to garnish

1 ▼ In a large bowl, combine the chicken, mint, lemon peel, lemon juice, 1 tablespoon of olive oil, ripe olives, salt, and lemon pepper. Leave to marinate at least 2 hours.

2 ▼ Form the mixture into four patties, pressing between your hands. Chill until ready to serve.

3 ▲ When ready to serve, cut the focaccia into quarters. Halve each quarter horizontally and liberally brush each half with olive oil. Toast under the broiler.

4 Brush the burgers on both sides with a little olive oil. Place on the broiler rack under the preheated hot broiler. Broil about 10 minutes, turning once, until thoroughly cooked through. To serve, place each burger between two pieces of focaccia and garnish with lettuce and lemon wedges.

BARBECUED CHICKEN

You need a bit of brute force to prepare the chicken, but once flattened it's an easy-and-tasty candidate for the barbecue.

SERVES 4

INGREDIENTS:
one 3-pound chicken
grated peel of 1 lemon
4 tbsp lemon juice
2 sprigs of rosemary
1 small red chili, seeded and finely
   chopped
⅔ cup olive oil

TO SERVE:
minted new potatoes
green salad

1 ▼ Split the chicken along the breastbone and open out, breaking the leg and wing joints in order to flatten the body.

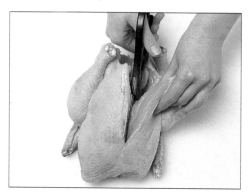

2 ▼ Cover with plastic wrap and pound to an even thickness with a rolling pin. This helps it cook evenly.

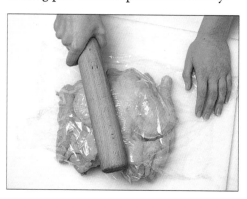

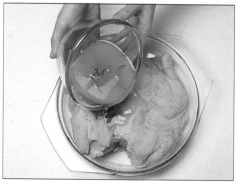

3 ▲ Mix the lemon peel and juice, rosemary sprigs, chili, and olive oil together in a small bowl. Place the chicken in a dish and pour the marinade over, turning the chicken to coat it evenly. Cover the dish and leave the chicken to marinate in the refrigerator at least 2 hours, or overnight. Let come to room temperature 30 minutes before grilling.

4 ▼ Cook the chicken over a hot barbecue (the coals should be white and red when fanned) about 30 minutes, turning it regularly until the skin is golden and crisp. To test if it is cooked, pierce one of the chicken thighs; if it is ready, the juices should run clear, not pink. Serve with minted new potatoes and a green salad.

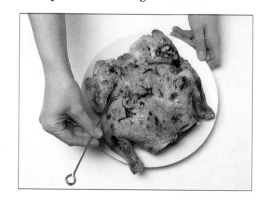

CHICKEN IN SPICY YOGURT

This dish is ideal for cooking on a barbecue, but make sure the barbecue is really hot. The coals should be white and glow red when fanned. You can also cook the chicken under a very hot broiler.

SERVES 6

INGREDIENTS:
3 dried red chilies
2 tbsp coriander seed
2 tsp turmeric
2 tsp garam masala or curry powder
4 garlic cloves, crushed
½ onion, chopped
1-inch piece fresh gingerroot, grated
2 tbsp lime juice
1 tsp salt
½ cup plain yogurt
1 tbsp oil
one 4-pound chicken, cut into 6 pieces, or 6 chicken portions

TO SERVE:
chopped tomatoes
diced cucumber
sliced red onion
Cucumber Raita (page 70)

1 Using a mortar and pestle, or an electric grinder, grind together the chilies, coriander, turmeric, garam masala, garlic, onion, ginger, lime juice, and salt.

2 ▼ Heat the spice paste in a skillet over low heat. Stir-fry about 2 minutes until fragrant. Pour into a shallow, nonporous bowl.

3 ▼ Stir the yogurt and oil into the spice paste.

4 Remove the skin from the chicken portions and make three slashes in the flesh of each piece. Add the chicken to the dish and make sure the pieces are coated in the marinade. Cover and chill at least 4 hours. Remove from the refrigerator and leave at room temperature, covered, 30 minutes before cooking.

5 Wrap the chicken pieces in foil, sealing well so the juices cannot escape. Cook the chicken pieces over a very hot barbecue about 15 minutes, turning once.

6 ▼ Using a pair of tongs, remove the the chicken from the foil. Brown the chicken on the barbecue 5 minutes. Serve with the chopped tomatoes, diced cucumber, sliced red onion, and the cucumber raita.

CHARGRILLED CHICKEN SALAD

This is a quick dish to serve at a barbecue while your hungry guests are waiting for the main event. If the bread is bent in half, the chicken salad can be put in the middle and eaten as finger food—remember to provide napkins!

SERVES 4

INGREDIENTS:
2 skinless, boneless chicken breast
  halves
1 red onion
oil for brushing
1 avocado, stoned
1 tbsp lemon juice
$1/2$ cup mayonnaise
$1/4$ tsp chili powder
$1/2$ tsp pepper
$1/4$ tsp salt
4 tomatoes, quartered
1 round sun-dried tomato-flavored
  focaccia bread
green salad, to serve

1 Cut the chicken breast halves into $1/2$-inch strips.

2 ▲ Cut the onion into eight pieces, held together at the root. Rinse under cold running water. Pat dry and brush with oil.

3 Purée or mash the avocado and lemon juice together. Whisk in the mayonnaise. Add the chili powder, pepper, and salt.

4 ▼ Put the chicken and onion over a hot barbecue. Grill 3 to 4 minutes on each side until beginning to blacken and cooked through.

5 Combine the blackened chicken and onion with the avocado mixture. Stir in the tomatoes.

6 ▲ Cut the focaccia in half twice to make quarter-shaped pieces. Slice each piece in half horizontally. Toast on the hot barbecue about 2 minutes on each side.

7 Spoon the chicken mixture over the toasts. Serve with a green salad.

MEDITERRANEAN GRILLED CHICKEN

Chargrilling and barbecuing over hot embers is a way of life in the Mediterranean countries. This recipe from the Languedoc area of France, uses crisp, juicy chicken.

SERVES 4

INGREDIENTS:
4 tbsp plain yogurt
3 tbsp sun-dried tomato paste
1 tbsp olive oil
¼ cup fresh basil leaves, lightly
  crushed
2 garlic cloves, roughly chopped
4 chicken quarters
coarse sea salt
green salad, to serve

1 ▼ Combine the yogurt, tomato paste, olive oil, basil leaves, and garlic in a small bowl and stir to mix.

2 ▼ Put the marinade into a bowl large enough to hold the chicken quarters in a single layer. Add the chicken quarters, stirring thoroughly to coat in the marinade.

3 Leave the chicken to marinate in the refrigerator at least 2 hours, or overnight. Remove and leave, covered, at room temperature 30 minutes before cooking.

4 ▼ Place the chicken quarters over a medium-hot barbecue and grill 30 to 40 minutes, turning frequently.

5 ▲ Test for doneness by piercing the flesh at the top of the drumstick. If the juices run clear, the chicken is cooked. If the juices are pink, cook 10 minutes longer.

6 Sprinkle with coarse sea salt. Serve hot with a green salad. This dish is also delicious eaten cold.

SPICY CHICKEN TIKKA

To prevent bamboo skewers charring during broiling, soak them in cold water 30 minutes before threading with the chicken.

SERVES 6

INGREDIENTS:
1 pound skinless, boneless chicken breast halves
1½ tbsp bottled tikka paste
6 tbsp plain yogurt
1 tbsp lemon juice
½ onion, finely chopped
1½ tbsp chopped chives or scallion tops
1½ tbsp finely chopped fresh gingerroot
1 or 2 garlic cloves, crushed
1½ tbsp sesame seeds
2 tbsp vegetable oil
lemon or lime juice for sprinkling
salt and pepper

1 Cut the chicken breasts into bite-sized pieces. Place in a shallow glass dish and season with salt and pepper to taste.

2 ▲ In a small bowl, mix together the remaining ingredients, except the sesame seeds, oil, and lemon or lime juice. Pour over the chicken. Stir until all the chicken pieces are coated. Cover and chill at least 1 hour, or longer if possible.

3 ▼ Thread the chicken pieces onto six bamboo or metal skewers. Sprinkle with the sesame seeds.

4 ▲ Place the skewers on the broiler rack and drizzle the chicken pieces with the oil. Broil about 15 minutes, or until the chicken is cooked through and browned, turning frequently and brushing with more oil, if necessary. Serve hot, sprinkled with lemon or lime juice.

CHICKEN TIKKA & MANGO KABOBS

Chicken tikka is one of the lower-fat dishes from India. Recipes vary but you can try your own combination of spices to suit your personal taste.

SERVES 4

INGREDIENTS:
four 4-ounce skinless, boneless chicken breast pieces
1 garlic clove, crushed
1 tsp grated fresh gingerroot
1 fresh green chili, seeded and finely chopped
6 tbsp low-fat plain yogurt
1 tbsp tomato paste
1 tsp ground cumin seeds
1 tsp ground coriander seeds
1 tsp ground turmeric
1 large ripe mango
2 tbsp lime juice
salt and pepper

TO GARNISH:
fresh cilantro leaves
lime wedges

TO SERVE:
boiled white rice
mixed salad
warmed naan bread

1 Cut the chicken into 1-inch cubes. Place in a shallow dish.

2 ▲ Mix together the garlic, ginger, chili, yogurt, tomato paste, cumin, coriander, turmeric, salt, and pepper. Spoon over the chicken and mix well. Cover and chill 2 hours.

3 Using a vegetable peeler, peel the skin from the mango. Slice down each side of the seed and cut the flesh into cubes. Toss in the lime juice. Cover and store in the refrigerator until required.

4 ▼ Thread the chicken and mango pieces onto eight skewers. Place on the broiler rack and brush with the yogurt marinade and any remaining lime juice.

5 Broil under medium heat 6 to 7 minutes. Turn over, brush again with the yogurt marinade and lime juice, and broil 6 to 7 minutes longer until the chicken juices run clear when the cubes are pierced with a sharp knife.

6 Serve on a bed of rice on a warmed platter with fresh cilantro leaves, lime wedges, a mixed salad, and warmed naan bread.

TANDOORI CHICKEN

The tandoor is a traditional Indian oven shaped like a huge urn. Charcoal is burnt slowly at the bottom until it becomes a mass of white-hot coals.

SERVES 4

INGREDIENTS:
8 small chicken portions, skinned
3 dried red chilies
1 tsp salt
2 tsp coriander seeds
2 tbsp lime juice
2 garlic cloves, crushed
1-inch piece fresh gingerroot, grated
1 clove
2 tsp garam masala
2 tsp chili powder
½ onion, chopped
1¼ cups plain yogurt
1 tbsp chopped fresh cilantro
lemon slices, to garnish

CUCUMBER RAITA:
1 cup plain yogurt
2 tsp chopped fresh mint
1½ cups cucumber, peeled, seeded, and cut into matchstick strips
salt

1 Using a sharp knife, make 2 or 3 slashes in the flesh of each chicken piece and place in a nonmetallic dish.

2 ▼ Crush the chilies, salt, coriander seeds, lime juice, garlic, ginger, and clove. Stir in the garam masala and chili powder. Transfer to a saucepan and heat gently until aromatic.

3 ▼ Remove the pan from the heat. Stir in the onion and yogurt.

4 Pour the yogurt mixture over the chicken. Cover and leave to marinate in the refrigerator at least 4 hours, or preferably overnight.

5 Combine the raita ingredients in a small bowl. Cover and chill.

6 Arrange the chicken pieces on the broiler pan. Broil under very hot heat, or grill over a barbecue, 20 to 30 minutes, turning once, until the juices run clear when the thickest parts of the portions are pierced with a sharp knife.

7 Sprinkle the chicken with chopped fresh cilantro. Serve hot or cold, garnished with the lemon slices and accompanied by cucumber raita.

SESAME SKEWERED CHICKEN
WITH GINGER BASTE

Chunks of chicken breast are marinated in a mixture of lime juice, garlic, sesame oil, and fresh ginger to give them a great flavor. The kabobs taste even more delicious if dipped into an accompanying bowl of hot chili sauce.

SERVES 4

INGREDIENTS:
1 pound boneless chicken breast halves
sprigs of fresh mint, to garnish

MARINADE:
1 garlic clove, crushed
1 shallot, chopped very finely
2 tbsp sesame oil
1 tbsp Thai fish sauce or light soy sauce
finely grated peel of 1 lime or ¹/₂ lemon
2 tbsp lime juice or lemon juice
1 tsp sesame seeds
2 tsp finely grated fresh gingerroot
2 tsp chopped fresh mint
salt and pepper

1 ▼ To make the marinade, put the garlic, shallot, sesame oil, fish sauce or soy sauce, lime or lemon peel and juice, sesame seeds, ginger, and chopped mint into a large nonmetallic bowl. Season to taste with a little salt and pepper.

2 ▼ Remove the skin from the chicken and cut the flesh into chunks. Add the chicken chunks to the marinade, stirring thoroughly to coat them in the mixture. Cover and chill in the refrigerator at least 2 hours, preferably longer. Meanwhile, soak 12 wooden skewers in warm water 30 minutes; this will prevent them from scorching during cooking.

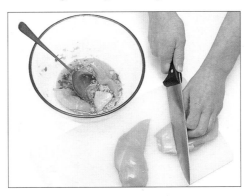

3 ▼ Thread the chicken onto the skewers. Place them in a foil-lined broiler pan. Liberally baste with the marinade.

4 Broil 8 to 10 minutes, turning the skewers frequently and basting the chicken with the remaining marinade. Serve at once, garnished with sprigs of fresh mint.

CRISPY CHICKEN DRUMSTICKS

Just the thing to put on the barbecue—chicken drumsticks, coated with a spicy, curry-like butter, grilled until crispy and golden. Serve with a green seasonal salad and rice.

SERVES 6

INGREDIENTS:
12 chicken drumsticks

SPICED BUTTER:
³/₄ cup butter
2 garlic cloves, crushed
1 tsp grated fresh gingerroot
2 tsp ground turmeric
4 tsp cayenne pepper
2 tbsp lime juice
3 tbsp mango chutney

TO SERVE:
green salad
boiled rice

1 Prepare a barbecue with medium coals, or preheat a conventional broiler to medium.

2 ▲ To make the spiced butter mixture, beat the butter with the garlic, ginger, turmeric, cayenne pepper, lime juice, and chutney until well blended.

3 ▼ Using a sharp knife, slash each chicken drumstick to the bone 3 or 4 times. Place the drumsticks on the rack under a hot broiler and broil 12 to 15 minutes until almost cooked, turning halfway through. Alternatively, cook over the barbecue 12 to 15 minutes.

4 ▲ Spread the chicken liberally with the spiced butter. Continue broiling or grilling 5 to 6 minutes longer, turning and basting frequently with the butter until golden and crisp.

5 Serve hot or at room temperature with a crisp green salad and rice.

CHICKEN SATAY KABOBS

Small kabobs of satay chicken with cubes of cheese and cherry tomatoes are served on crisp lettuce leaves. These are ideal to serve as an appetizer or take on a picnic.

MAKES 8

INGREDIENTS:
1 tbsp sherry
1 tbsp light soy sauce
1 tbsp sesame oil
finely grated peel of ¹/₂ lemon
1 tbsp lemon or lime juice
2 tsp sesame seeds
1 pound skinless, boneless chicken breast halves
3 ounces Gouda cheese, or similar hard cheese
16 cherry tomatoes
crisp lettuce leaves
salt and pepper

PEANUT DIP:
¹/₃ cup shredded coconut
²/₃ cup boiling water
¹/₂ cup crunchy peanut butter
good pinch of chili powder
1 tsp brown sugar
1 tbsp light soy sauce
2 scallions, trimmed and chopped finely

1 In a bowl, combine the sherry, soy sauce, sesame oil, lemon peel, lemon or lime juice, sesame seeds, salt, and pepper.

2 Cut the chicken into 1-inch cubes. Add to the marinade and stir well. Cover and leave to chill in the refrigerator 3 to 6 hours.

3 To make the dip, put the coconut in a saucepan with the boiling water. Bring back to a boil; set aside until cool. Add the peanut butter, chili powder, sugar, and soy sauce. Bring slowly to a boil. Simmer very gently, stirring all the time, 2 to 3 minutes until thickened. Remove from the heat and leave to cool. Meanwhile, soak eight wooden skewers in warm water 30 minutes.

4 ▲ Stir the scallions into the peanut mixture. Spoon into a serving bowl; set aside.

5 Thread the marinaded chicken pieces onto the skewers, positioning them in the middle. Broil under a medium broiler about 5 minutes on each side until cooked through. Leave until cool.

6 ▼ Cut the cheese into 16 cubes. Thread one cheese cube and a cherry tomato onto each end of the skewers.

7 To serve, arrange each kabob on a crisp lettuce leaf and serve with the peanut dip.

BLACKENED CHICKEN WITH GUACAMOLE

This easy recipe is typical of French Cajun cooking, which has its roots in earthy, strong flavors, and uses plenty of spices. The dish includes a typical Cajun spice mix.

SERVES 4

INGREDIENTS:
*4 skinless, boneless chicken breast
    halves
4 tbsp butter, melted*

CAJUN SPICE MIXTURE:
*1 tsp salt
1 tbsp sweet paprika
1 tsp dried onion granules
1 tsp dried garlic granules
1 tsp dried thyme
1 tsp cayenne
1/2 tsp cracked black pepper
1/2 tsp dried oregano*

GUACAMOLE:
*1 avocado
1 tbsp lemon juice
2 tbsp sour cream
1/2 red onion, chopped
1 garlic clove, halved*

1 Put the chicken pieces between two pieces of plastic wrap and pound with a mallet or rolling pin to an even thickness. They should be about 1½ inches thick.

2 ▼ Brush each chicken piece all over with the melted butter; set aside.

3 Combine the spice mix ingredients in a shallow bowl.

4 ▲ Dip the chicken pieces in the spice mix, patting it on so both sides are completely coated; set aside.

5 To make the guacamole, mash the avocado thoroughly with the lemon juice in a small bowl. Stir in the sour cream and red onion.

6 ▼ Wipe the garlic clove around the guacamole dish, pressing hard. Spoon in the guacamole; cover and set aside.

7 Place the chicken over the hottest part of a very hot barbecue and grill 8 to 10 minutes, turning once.

8 Slice the chicken into thick pieces. Serve immediately accompanied by the guacamole.

JERK CHICKEN

This is a popular Caribbean dish. Rubbing pastes and "rubs" into meat, poultry or seafood is a technique first introduced by the Arawak Indians. It helps to tenderize the meat.

SERVES 6

INGREDIENTS:
3 pounds chicken pieces
cherry tomatoes, to garnish
salad, to serve

MARINADE:
6 scallions
2 fresh red chilies, preferably Scotch bonnet
2 tbsp dark soy sauce
2 tbsp lime juice
3 tsp ground allspice
1/2 tsp ground bay leaves
1 tsp ground cinnamon
2 garlic cloves, chopped
2 tsp brown sugar
1 tsp dried thyme
1/2 tsp salt

1 ▼ To make the marinade, chop the scallions. Seed and chop the fresh red chilies.

2 Put the scallions, chilies, and the remaining marinade ingredients into a food processor. Blend until smooth. Alternatively, chop the scallions and chilies very finely (being careful not to touch your eyes). Add these to the remaining ingredients and, using a mortar and pestle, work into a chunky paste.

3 ▼ Place the chicken pieces in a shallow dish and generously spoon the marinade over. Cover and put into the refrigerator to marinate 24 hours, turning each piece of chicken several times to make sure it is evenly marinated.

4 ▲ Brush the broiler rack with oil. Place the chicken pieces on top. Broil under a medium-hot broiler 15 to 20 minutes on each side until the juices run clear when the thickest part of the flesh is pierced with a sharp knife.

FILIPINO CHICKEN

Tomato catsup is used in this recipe from the Philippines. It is a very popular ingredient as it has a zingy sweet-sour flavor.

SERVES 4

INGREDIENTS:
1 can lemonade or lime-and-lemonade
2 tbsp gin
4 tbsp tomato catsup
2 tsp garlic salt
2 tsp Worcestershire sauce
4 skinless chicken breast halves
salt and pepper

TO SERVE:
Chinese thread egg noodles
1 green chili, finely chopped
2 scallions, sliced

1 ▼ Combine the lemonade or lime-and-lemonade, gin, tomato catsup, garlic salt, Worcestershire sauce, and seasoning in a large, nonporous dish.

2 ▼ Add the chicken pieces into the dish, stirring until they are covered.

3 Cover and leave to marinate in the refrigerator 2 hours. Remove and allow to come to room temperature 30 minutes before cooking.

4 ▲ Cook the chicken pieces over a medium-hot barbecue 20 minutes, turning once, until completely cooked through.

5 Remove the chicken pieces from the barbecue and leave to rest 3 to 4 minutes.

6 Carve into thin slices. Serve with egg noodles, tossed with a little green chili and scallions.

THAI CHICKEN WITH PEANUT SAUCE

This is a favourite Thai dish served with a spicy peanut sauce. It can be made with chicken or beef.

SERVES 4 TO 6

INGREDIENTS:
*4 skinless, boneless chicken breast
  halves*

MARINADE:
*1 small onion, finely chopped
1 garlic clove, crushed
1-inch piece fresh gingerroot, grated
2 tbsp dark soy sauce
2 tsp chili powder
1 tsp ground coriander seeds
2 tsp dark brown sugar
1 tbsp lemon or lime juice
1 tbsp vegetable oil*

SPICY PEANUT SAUCE:
*1¼ cups coconut milk
⅓ cup crunchy peanut butter
1 tbsp Thai fish sauce
1 tsp lemon or lime juice
salt and pepper*

1 Trim any fat from the chicken pieces. Cut them into thin strips, about 3 inches long.

2 ▼ To make the marinade, place all the ingredients in a shallow dish and stir well. Add the chicken strips and stir in the marinade until well coated. Cover and put in the refrigerator to marinate at least 2 hours, or overnight. Meanwhile, soak six wooden skewers 30 minutes.

3 ▼ Remove the chicken from the marinade and thread the pieces, concertina style, onto the skewers.

4 Broil the chicken skewers 8 to 10 minutes, turning and brushing occasionally with the marinade, until cooked through and tender.

5 ▼ Meanwhile, to make the spicy peanut sauce, mix the coconut milk with the peanut butter, fish sauce, and lemon or lime juice in a saucepan. Bring to a boil and boil 3 minutes. Season with salt and pepper to taste. Pour into a serving bowl and serve with the chicken.

CRISPY-COATED SQUAB CHICKENS

You could adapt this recipe using a whole chicken or chicken pieces, serving them on the bed of moist and colorful vegetables.

SERVES 6

INGREDIENTS:
4 tbsp vegetable oil
4 tbsp butter
6 squab chickens, trussed
1 large onion, sliced
1 pound baby carrots
1 tbsp flour
2/3 cup white wine
juice of 2 oranges
2 fennel bulbs, quartered
1 1/4 cups chicken stock
1/2 tsp salt
1 tbsp black peppercorns, lightly crushed
1 tsp cornstarch
2/3 cup plain yogurt
salt and pepper

COATING:
3 tbsp brown crystal sugar
1 tbsp black peppercorns, lightly crushed
3 tbsp coarse sea salt
2/3 cup plain yogurt

1 ▼ Heat the oil in a large heavy-bottomed flameproof casserole. Add the butter. When bubbling, add the squab chickens in batches and brown evenly on all sides. Remove from the pan and keep warm.

2 Add the onion to the pan and fry until translucent. Add the carrots, stir to coat evenly, then sprinkle on the flour and blend well. Pour in the wine and orange juice, stirring all the time. Add the fennel, chicken stock, salt, and peppercorns. Bring to a boil. Pour into a large roasting pan.

3 ▲ Arrange the squab chickens in the roasting pan and cover with foil. Cook in a preheated oven, 350°F, 40 minutes.

4 To make the coating, stir together the sugar, peppercorns, salt, and yogurt to make a thick paste.

5 ▼ Remove the squab chickens from the roasting pan and place on the broiler rack. Spread the yogurt coating evenly over each chicken. Broil under a hot broiler 3 to 4 minutes until crisp and browned.

6 Remove the vegetables in the pan with a draining spoon and place on a warm serving dish. Place the pan over medium heat and bring the pan juices to a boil. Stir the cornstarch into the yogurt, then blend into the pan juices. Check the seasoning. Place the chickens on the serving dish and spoon a little sauce over. Serve the remaining sauce separately.

SQUAB CHICKENS WITH GREEN PEPPERCORNS

Squab chickens are a great alternative to ordinary chicken. One bird serves two people and can be cooked whole.

SERVES 4

INGREDIENTS:
2 squab chickens, halved lengthwise
2 tbsp oil
2 tbsp butter
1 onion, chopped
3 tbsp bottled green peppercorns, drained
2 tbsp coarse-grain mustard
½ cup white wine
1 cup basmati and wild rice, mixed
2 cups chicken stock
salt and pepper
sautéd cherry tomatoes, to serve
sprigs of fresh thyme, to garnish

1 ▼ Wash the chicken halves and pat dry. Season well with salt and pepper.

2 ▼ Heat the oil and butter in a skillet. Add the onions and fry 5 minutes until soft. Add the chickens and fry until evenly browned.

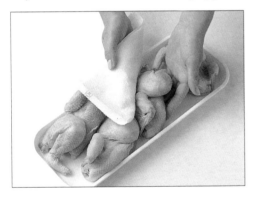

3 Transfer the browned chicken halves from the skillet to a roasting pan. Roast in a preheated oven, 400°F, about 30 minutes.

4 ▲ Meanwhile, stir the peppercorns, mustard, and wine into the juices in the skillet. Bring to a boil and boil until reduced by half.

5 ▼ Stir in the rice, and pour on the chicken stock. Season well and bring to a boil. Reduce the heat and simmer 18 to 20 minutes. Adjust the seasoning, if necessary.

6 Serve the chickens with rice, accompanied by sautéd tomatoes. Garnish with a sprig of thyme.

TRADITIONAL ROAST CHICKEN

Roast chicken is an all-time classic which pleases everyone.

SERVES 4 TO 6

INGREDIENTS:
4 slices bacon
8 small link sausages
1 roasting chicken, about 4 pounds, with giblets
4 tbsp butter
2 pounds potatoes
watercress, to garnish

STUFFING:
2 ounces white crustless bread
4 ounces ground pork sausage meat
1 tbsp chopped mixed fresh herbs
1 tbsp chopped fresh sage
chicken livers from the giblets, washed and dried

BREAD SAUCE:
1¼ cups milk
3 ounces crustless white bread
1 onion pierced with 10 cloves
2 tbsp butter
pinch of ground allspice
1 tbsp heavy cream
1 tbsp all-purpose flour
⅔ cup chicken stock
2 to 3 tbsp sherry

1 ▼ Cut the bacon in half widthwise, and stretch with the back of a knife. Wrap each piece around a small pork sausage; set aside.

2 Wash and dry the breast cavity of the chicken; set aside.

3 To make the stuffing, turn on the food processor and insert the bread through the feed tube. Process until finely crumbed. Now add the sausage meat, mixed herbs, sage, and chicken livers. Alternatively, grate the bread to form crumbs, chop the livers, and mash together with the other stuffing ingredients.

4 Spoon the stuffing into the neck end of the bird, using the loose skin to make a pocket of stuffing, filling out the breast.

5 ▲ Close the flap of skin underneath the chicken, using string or skewers. Put any remaining stuffing in the body cavity.

6 Transfer the chicken to a roasting pan and pat the butter all over. Cover loosely with baking parchment and bake in a preheated oven, 400°F, 20 minutes.

7 Meanwhile, cut the potatoes into an even size. Parboil in salted boiling water, then drain. Spoon in the potatoes around the chicken, turning to coat in the fat.

8 Reduce the heat to 350°F and bake 80 minutes, basting the chicken at least three times. Add the sausages after 50 minutes. Remove the baking parchment 15 minutes before the end of roasting time. Transfer the potatoes to a serving dish when they are browned and crisp.

9 Meanwhile, to make the sauce, put all the ingredients in a saucepan and simmer 30 minutes. Discard the onion. Set the sauce aside and keep warm.

10 Remove the chicken from the oven and leave to rest in a warm place for 20 minutes while you make the gravy. Arrange the potatoes and sausages around the chicken, and garnish with watercress. Serve with the bread sauce.

CASSEROLES

Braising or casseroling is one of the classic methods of cooking chicken, producing the most delectable results. The chicken is simmered in a sealed casserole with aromatic vegetables and herbs and a small amount of liquid. Cooked on the stovetop over the lowest possible heat, or in a low oven, chicken becomes meltingly tender, moistened by the enriched juices. One of the most celebrated classic casseroles is the French Coq au Vin, here made with white wine instead of the more traditional red. Other lip-smacking favorites include Chicken with 40 Garlic Cloves from France, Baton Rouge Gumbo Chicken from New Orleans, and Chicken Cacciatora from Italy.

ROMAN CHICKEN (PAGE 87)

CHICKEN CACCIATORA

In this popular Italian classic, browned chicken quarters are cooked in a tomato-and-pepper sauce.

SERVES 4

🐘🐘🐘🐘🐘🐘🐘🐘🐘🐘🐘🐘🐘🐘

INGREDIENTS:
1 roasting chicken, about 3 pounds, cut into 6 or 8 serving pieces
1 cup all-purpose flour
3 tbsp olive oil
⅔ cup dry white wine
1 green bell pepper, seeded and sliced
1 red bell pepper, seeded and sliced
1 carrot, finely chopped
1 celery stalk, finely chopped
1 garlic clove, crushed
1 can (8-ounce) crushed tomatoes
salt and pepper

🐘🐘🐘🐘🐘🐘🐘🐘🐘🐘🐘🐘🐘🐘

1 ▼ Rinse and pat dry the chicken pieces with paper towels. Lightly dust them with seasoned flour.

2 ▼ Heat the oil in a large skillet. Add the chicken and fry over medium heat until browned all over. Remove from the pan; set aside.

3 ▼ Drain off all but 2 tablespoons of the fat in the pan. Add the wine and stir for a few minutes. Add the peppers, carrots, celery, and garlic. Season well and simmer together about 15 minutes.

4 ▼ Return the chicken to the pan and add the crushed tomatoes. Cover and simmer 30 minutes, stirring often, until the chicken is cooked through.

5 Check the seasoning before serving piping hot.

CHICKEN WITH 40 GARLIC CLOVES

In France, the chicken is served accompanied by slices of bread. Each diner spreads the bread with the softened and sweetened garlic.

SERVES 4

INGREDIENTS:
*1 roasting chicken, weighing about
  3 pounds
2 tbsp fresh thyme leaves
2 tbsp fresh rosemary needles
2 tbsp fresh sage leaves
2 tbsp fresh parsley leaves
2 small celery stalks
40 fresh garlic cloves, unpeeled
4 tbsp olive oil
salt*

1 ▲ Rinse the chicken and pat dry. Rub salt into the skin.

2 ▼ Stuff the cavity with half of the fresh herbs, one celery stalk, and 10 of the garlic cloves.

3 ▲ Place the chicken in a roasting pan or earthenware dish with the rest of the herbs, celery, and garlic. Brush the olive oil all over the skin.

4 Roast in a preheated oven, 400°F, 1½ hours, basting frequently.

5 Transfer the cooked chicken to a warmed serving platter, and surround with the cloves of garlic. Skim off most of the fat from the cooking juices. Bring the juices to a boil and reduce slightly. Strain into a warmed gravy boat to serve.

CHICKEN & BLACK-EYED PEAS

In India and Pakistan, legumes are a valuable source of nourishment in mountainous areas in winter when meat is scarce. You can use any variety of legume in this spicy dish; just alter the cooking times accordingly.

SERVES 4

INGREDIENTS:

*generous 1 cup dried black-eyed peas,
    soaked overnight and drained*
1 tsp salt
2 onions, chopped
2 garlic cloves, crushed
1 tsp ground turmeric
1 tsp ground cumin
*one 2¹/₂-pound chicken, jointed into
    8 pieces*
*1 green bell pepper, seeded and
    chopped*
2 tbsp oil
*1-inch piece fresh gingerroot,
    grated*
2 tsp coriander seeds
¹/₂ tsp fennel seeds
*2 tsp garam masala or curry
    powder*
*1 tbsp chopped fresh cilantro, to
    garnish*

1 ▼ Put the drained peas into a wok or large skillet with the salt, onions, garlic, turmeric, and cumin. Cover with water. Bring to a boil and boil 15 minutes.

2 Add the chicken and bell pepper to the wok. Return to a boil. Lower the heat and simmer 30 minutes until the juices run clear when the thickest parts of the chicken pieces are pierced with a sharp knife.

3 ▼ Heat the oil in a clean wok. Add the ginger, coriander seeds, and fennel seeds and fry 30 seconds.

4 ▼ Stir the ginger, coriander seeds, and fennel seeds into the chicken. Add the garam masala. Simmer 5 minutes longer. Serve garnished with chopped fresh cilantro.

CHICKEN & CHILI BEAN POT

This aromatic Mexican chicken dish has a spicy kick. Chicken thighs are more economical than breasts, but you can also use four large breast halves if you prefer.

SERVES 4

INGREDIENTS:
2 tbsp all-purpose flour
1 tsp chili powder
8 chicken thighs or 4 chicken legs
3 tbsp olive or vegetable oil
2 garlic cloves, crushed
1 large onion, chopped
1 green or red bell pepper, seeded and chopped
1¼ cups chicken stock
12 ounces tomatoes, chopped
1 can (14-ounce) red kidney beans, rinsed and drained
2 tbsp tomato paste
salt and pepper

1 ▼ Mix together the flour, chili powder, salt, and pepper in a shallow dish. Rinse the chicken, but do not dry. Dip the chicken into the seasoned flour, coating it on all sides.

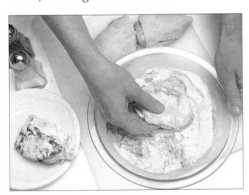

2 ▲ Heat the oil in a large, deep skillet or saucepan. Add the chicken pieces and fry over high heat 3 to 4 minutes, turning the pieces so they are browned all over. Remove from the pan with a draining spoon and drain on paper towels.

3 Add the garlic, onion, and bell pepper to the pan and fry 2 to 3 minutes until softened.

4 ▼ Add the stock, tomatoes, kidney beans, and tomato paste, stirring well. Bring to a boil.

5 Return the chicken to the pan. Reduce the heat and simmer, covered, about 30 minutes, until the chicken is tender and cooked through. Season to taste. Transfer to a warm serving dish and serve at once.

CHICKEN WITH GREEN OLIVES

Olives are a popular flavoring for poultry and game in Italy, where this recipe originates. The Italians use every bit of the bird in some way, most often for soups and stock.

SERVES 4

INGREDIENTS:
4 chicken breast halves, part boned
2 tbsp olive oil
2 tbsp butter
1 large onion, finely chopped
2 garlic cloves, crushed
2 red, yellow, or green bell peppers,
    seeded and cut into large pieces
2½ cups sliced or quartered large
    closed-cap mushrooms,
6 ounces tomatoes, peeled and
    halved
⅔ cup dry white wine
⅔ to 1 cup green olives, stoned
4 to 6 tbsp heavy cream
salt and pepper
chopped flat-leafed parsley,
    to garnish
boiled pasta, to serve

1 Season the chicken with salt and pepper. Heat the oil and butter in a large skillet. Add the chicken and fry until browned all over. Remove from the pan and keep warm.

2 ▼ Add the onion and garlic to the pan and fry gently until beginning to soften. Add the bell peppers and the mushrooms and continue to cook a few minutes longer.

3 ▲ Stir the tomatoes and plenty of seasoning into the pan. Transfer the vegetable mixture to a flameproof casserole. Arrange the chicken on the bed of vegetables.

4 Add the wine to the skillet and bring to a boil. Pour the wine over the chicken. Cover the casserole and cook in a preheated oven, 350°F, 50 minutes.

5 ▼ Stir the olives into the chicken. Pour in the cream. Re-cover the casserole and return to the oven 10 to 20 minutes, or until the chicken is very tender and cooked through.

6 Adjust the seasoning. Serve the pieces of chicken, surrounded by the vegetables and sauce, with boiled pasta. Sprinkle with chopped parsley to garnish.

ROMAN CHICKEN

This Roman dish is equally good cold and can be taken on a picnic—serve with bread to mop up the juices.

SERVES 4

INGREDIENTS:
4 tbsp olive oil
6 chicken pieces
4 large mixed red, green, and yellow bell peppers
1 large red onion, sliced
2 garlic cloves, crushed with 1 tsp salt
²/₃ cup stoned green olives
Tomato Sauce (page 43)
1¹/₄ cups hot chicken stock
2 sprigs fresh marjoram
salt and pepper

1 ▼ Heat half the oil in a flameproof casserole. Add the chicken pieces and brown on all sides. Remove the chicken pieces; set aside.

2 ▼ Remove the seeds and the cores from the bell peppers and cut them into strips.

3 ▲ Add the remaining oil to the casserole. Fry the onion gently 5 to 7 minutes until just softened. Add the crushed garlic and fry a minute longer. Stir in the bell peppers, olives, and tomato sauce and bring to a boil.

4 ▼ Return the chicken to the casserole. Add the stock and the marjoram. Cover the casserole and simmer gently about 45 minutes until the chicken is tender. Season to taste with salt and pepper. Serve with warm crusty bread.

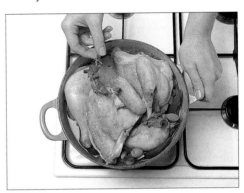

COQ AU VIN BLANC

Small pieces of chicken are gently simmered with wine, herbs, bacon, mushrooms, and onions to produce a dish reminiscent of an authentic French meal.

SERVES 2

INGREDIENTS:
2 chicken quarters
4 slices thick, lean slab bacon, rinded if
*   necessary*
2 tbsp oil
4 ounces pearl onions, or 1 large onion,
*   sliced*
1 garlic clove, crushed
2/3 cup dry white wine
1 1/4 cups chicken stock
1 bay leaf
large pinch of dried oregano
1 tbsp cornstarch
3/4 cup tiny button mushrooms, trimmed
salt and pepper
chopped fresh parsley, to garnish
boiled rice or creamed potatoes,
*   to serve*

1 ▼ Cut each chicken quarter into two pieces and season well with salt and pepper. Cut the bacon slices into ½ inch strips.

2 Heat the oil in a large saucepan. Add the chicken and fry until golden brown. Remove from the pan. Add the bacon, onions, and garlic and fry until lightly browned. Drain off all the fat from the saucepan.

3 ▼ Add the wine, stock, bay leaf, oregano, salt, and pepper to the saucepan. Return the chicken to the pan and bring to a boil.

4 Cover the saucepan tightly and reduce the heat. Simmer very gently 40 to 50 minutes, or until the chicken is very tender and cooked through.

5 ▲ Blend the cornstarch with a little cold water. Add to the saucepan with the mushrooms. Return to a boil. Simmer 5 minutes longer.

6 Adjust the seasoning and discard the bay leaf. Serve sprinkled liberally with chopped parsley, accompanied by boiled rice or creamed potatoes.

COUNTRY CHICKEN CASSEROLE

Most ceramic casserole dishes can be used with care on the stovetop, but a piece of equipment called a diffuser (usually a double layer of perforated metal holding the dish off the heat) should be placed between the heat and the dish. However, if you are unsure, simply sauté the chicken and transfer to an ovenproof serving dish.

SERVES 4

INGREDIENTS:

1 free-range chicken, about 3 pounds,
    cut into 6 to 8 pieces
flour for dusting
2 tbsp butter
1 tsp olive oil
10 pearl onions
3 garlic cloves, unpeeled
1 carrot, diced
1 celery stalk, diced
1 bay leaf
4 ounces smoked bacon,
    diced
2½ cups stock, or to cover
1½ pounds new potatoes,
    sliced
salt and pepper

1 ▲ Rinse and pat dry the chicken. Dust with flour. Melt the butter with the oil in a flameproof casserole over medium-high heat. Add the chicken pieces and brown all over; set aside.

2 ▲ Add the onions, garlic, carrot, celery, bay leaf, and bacon to the casserole. Cook over medium heat 10 minutes. Season well. Return the chicken to the casserole. Pour in the stock. Check the seasoning.

3 ▼ Arrange the sliced potatoes over the top of the chicken and vegetables. Cover and simmer 1 hour.

4 Serve piping hot with a green vegetable.

CHICKEN WITH RICE & PEAS

This dish, which is also known as chicken pelau, is a national favorite in Trinidad and Tobago. The secret of a good pelau is that it must be brown in color, which is achieved by caramelizing the chicken.

SERVES 6

INGREDIENTS:
1 onion, chopped
2 garlic cloves
1 tbsp chopped fresh chives
1 tbsp chopped fresh thyme
2 celery stalks with leaves, chopped
1½ cups water
½ fresh coconut, chopped
liquid from 1 fresh coconut
1 can (16-ounce) pigeon peas or kidney
*   beans, drained*
1 red chili, seeded and thinly sliced
2 tbsp peanut oil
2 tbsp sugar
3 pounds chicken pieces
1¼ cups white long-grain rice, rinsed
*   and drained*
salt and pepper
celery leaves, to garnish

1 Put the onion, garlic, chives, thyme, celery, and 4 tablespoons of the water into a food processor and blend until smooth. Alternatively, chop the onion and celery very finely, then grind with the garlic and herbs in a pestle and mortar, gradually mixing in the water. Pour into a saucepan; set aside.

to a thick milk, adding water if necessary. Alternatively, finely grate the coconut and mix with the liquid. Add to the onion and celery mixture.

3 Stir in the drained pigeon peas or kidney beans and chili. Cook over low heat 15 minutes. Season to taste with salt and pepper.

5 Add the chicken and cook 15 to 20 minutes, turning frequently, until browned all over.

6 ▲ Stir in the coconut mixture, the rice, and the remaining water. Bring to a boil. Reduce the heat, cover, and simmer 20 minutes until the chicken and rice are tender and the liquid has been absorbed. Garnish with celery leaves and serve.

2 ▲ Put the chopped coconut and liquid into the food processor and mix

4 ▲ Put the oil and sugar in a heavy-bottomed flameproof casserole and cook over medium heat until the sugar begins to caramelize.

CHICKEN & VEGETABLE RICE

Boneless chicken breast halves can be used instead of the drumsticks, but they should be slashed diagonally.

SERVES 4 TO 6

INGREDIENTS:
4 chicken drumsticks
3 tbsp mango chutney
1¹/₂ tbsp lemon juice
6 tbsp vegetable oil
1 to 2 tbsp medium or hot curry paste
1¹/₂ tsp paprika
1 large onion, chopped
4 ounces button mushrooms
2 carrots, thinly sliced
2 celery sticks, trimmed and thinly sliced
¹/₂ eggplant, quartered and sliced
2 garlic cloves, crushed
¹/₂ tsp ground cinnamon
1¹/₄ cups long-grain rice
2¹/₂ cups chicken stock or water
¹/₂ cup frozen peas or sliced green beans
¹/₃ cup seedless raisins
salt and pepper

TO GARNISH:
hard-cooked egg slices
lemon slices (optional)

1 ▼ Slash the drumsticks twice on each side, cutting through the skin and deep into the flesh. Mix the chutney with the lemon juice, 1 tablespoon of the oil, the curry paste, and paprika. Brush over the drumsticks and reserve the remainder for later.

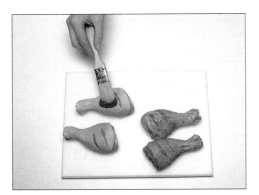

2 Heat 2 tablespoons of oil in a skillet. Add the drumsticks and fry about 5 minutes until sealed and golden brown all over.

3 ▲ Meanwhile, heat the remaining oil in a saucepan. Add the onion, mushrooms, carrots, celery, eggplant, garlic, and cinnamon and fry 1 minute. Stir in the rice and cook 1 minute, stirring until the rice is coated with the oil. Add the stock and the remaining mango chutney mixture, peas, raisins, and seasoning. Stir and bring to a boil.

4 ▼ Reduce the heat and add the drumsticks to the mixture, pushing them down into the liquid. Cover and simmer 25 minutes until the liquid is absorbed, the drumsticks are tender and the rice is cooked.

5 Remove the drumsticks from the pan and keep warm. Fluff up the rice mixture and transfer to a warm serving plate. Arrange the rice in a mound and place the drumsticks around it. Garnish the dish with wedges of hard-cooked egg and lemon slices, if using.

JAMBALAYA

Jambalaya, New Orleans' version of paella, dates from the 18th century, when it was served as slave food. Today, this hearty dish can contain any number of meats, including chicken, duck, ham, or sausage.

SERVES 4

INGREDIENTS:
4 tbsp butter
2 onions, chopped
2 garlic cloves, crushed
5 celery stalks, chopped
1 red bell pepper, seeded and chopped
1 green bell pepper, seeded and chopped
1 tsp Cajun Spice Mixture (page 74)
1¼ cups long-grain rice
1 can (14-ounce) tomatoes, drained and chopped
1 pound assorted cooked meats, such as chicken, duck, ham, or sausage, sliced or diced
1 cup vegetable stock or white wine
1 tsp salt
parsley sprigs, to garnish

1 Melt the butter in a large, flameproof casserole. Add the onions, garlic, celery, bell peppers, and Cajun spice mixture and mix well.

2 ▲ Add the rice and stir well to coat the grains in the butter mixture.

3 ▼ Add the tomatoes, meats, stock or wine, and salt. Bring to a boil, stirring well.

4 Reduce the heat, cover, and simmer about 15 minutes, or until the rice is cooked and fluffy and has absorbed all the liquid. If the mixture seems to be too dry, add a little boiling water, tablespoon by tablespoon, toward the end of the cooking time.

5 Serve the jamabalaya on warm plates, garnished with parsley.

BATON ROUGE CHICKEN GUMBO

It seems that everyone in the state of Louisiana has their favorite recipe for gumbo. This one uses chicken with shrimp, okra, and a little pork belly—a traditional recipe for this famous dish that is difficult to improve upon.

SERVES 4 TO 6

INGREDIENTS:

2 tbsp butter
1 tbsp corn oil
¼ cup all-purpose flour
3 ounces pork belly, sliced
1 large onion, sliced
2 celery stalks, chopped
3 cups trimmed and sliced okra
1 can (14-ounce) peeled tomatoes
2 garlic cloves, crushed
4½ cups chicken stock or water
8 ounces peeled cooked shrimp
1 pound skinless cooked chicken, cut into bite-sized pieces
1 tsp hot-pepper sauce
3 cups hot cooked rice, to serve

1 ▼ Heat the butter and oil in a small, heavy-bottomed pan. Add the flour and cook, stirring frequently, over low heat until the roux turns a rich brown color; set aside.

2 Meanwhile, in a large pan, fry the pork slices, without extra fat, until they are golden brown on all sides and the fat has been rendered. Add the sliced onion and celery and cook 5 minutes longer.

3 ▼ Stir in the okra and fry gently 3 minutes longer. Stir in the tomatoes and garlic and simmer over low heat 15 minutes.

4 Gradually add the stock to the browned roux, stirring and blending well. Add to the okra mixture. Cover and simmer 1 hour.

5 ▲ Add the shrimp and chicken to the pork and vegetable mixture. Cook 5 minutes longer until the chicken is thoroughly reheated. Stir in the hot-pepper sauce.

6 Spoon the gumbo into individual serving bowls and top with a scoop of hot cooked rice.

CHICKEN ETOUFFE

Etouffé means smothered and is a popular way of presenting food in Cajun cuisine. Here, strips of chicken and vegetables are smothered in a thickened dark sauce flavored with basil.

SERVES 4 TO 6

INGREDIENTS:
4 tbsp butter
1 small onion, chopped
1 celery stalk, chopped
1 small green bell pepper, seeded and chopped
1 red bell pepper, seeded and chopped
1 small red chili, seeded and finely chopped
1 tsp Cajun Spice Mixture (page 74)
1 tsp chopped fresh basil
2 tbsp vegetable oil
2 tbsp all-purpose flour
2 cups rich chicken stock
1 pound skinless, boneless chicken breasts, cut into strips or bite-sized pieces
4 scallions, chopped
salt
couscous or rice, to serve

1 ▼ Melt the butter in a large, heavy-bottomed flameproof casserole. Add the onion, celery, green and red bell peppers, and chili and cook over low heat about 5 minutes, stirring from time to time, until softened.

2 Add the Cajun spice mixture, basil and salt. Cook for a further 2 minutes.

3 Meanwhile, heat the oil in a pan. Add the flour and cook, slowly, until a rich reddish-brown roux is formed. Whisk constantly to prevent the roux from scorching and becoming bitter.

4 ▼ Gradually add the stock and whisk to make a smooth, thickened sauce. Pour the sauce over the vegetable mixture and leave to simmer about 15 minutes.

5 ▼ Add the chicken strips or pieces and the scallions to the pan and cook 10 minutes longer, stirring occasionally, until the chicken is cooked through and tender.

6 Serve with freshly cooked fluffy couscous or cooked long-grain rice.

GRILLADES WITH GRITS

Grillades is a Cajun meat and vegetable stew in a thick gravy. It is considered to be Bayou breakfast food and would always be served with grits, a creamy cereal made from corn. Couscous is a good alternative.

SERVES 6

INGREDIENTS:

4 tbsp olive oil
2 pounds skinless, boneless chicken breast halves, cut into 3- × 4-inch strips
$^{1}/_{2}$ cup all-purpose flour
3 onions, chopped
2 green bell peppers, seeded and chopped
4 celery stalks, finely chopped
1 garlic clove, crushed
3 cups peeled, seeded, and chopped ripe tomatoes
2 tbsp tomato paste
1 tsp chopped fresh thyme
$^{1}/_{2}$ to 1 tsp hot-pepper sauce
$1^{1}/_{2}$ tsp paprika
$^{1}/_{4}$ tsp cayenne pepper
1 tsp salt
$^{2}/_{3}$ cup vegetable stock
$^{2}/_{3}$ cup white wine
hominy grits or couscous, to serve

1 ▼ Heat the oil in a heavy-bottomed skillet. Add the chicken strips and fry quickly on both sides until no longer pink. Remove with a draining spoon; set aside.

2 ▼ Add the flour to the pan juices and stir until the flour is absorbed by the juices. Cook over medium heat, stirring constantly, until the roux changes to a rich brown color.

3 Add the onions, bell peppers, celery, and garlic and stir. Cover and cook over low heat about 15 minutes until softened.

4 ▲ Return the chicken to the pan with the tomatoes, tomato paste, thyme, hot-pepper sauce, paprika, cayenne, salt, stock, and wine. Stir together.

5 Cover and simmer 40 to 45 minutes longer, or until the chicken and vegetables are cooked. Serve the grillades hot with hominy grits, if liked, or with couscous.